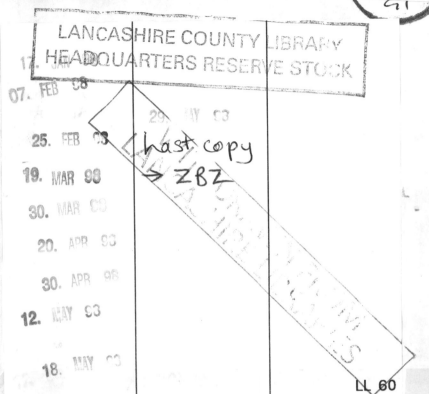

AN AIRMAN'S LOT

Leonard L Bridge

NEWTON

First Published in Great Britain by
Newton Publishers (1995)
P.O.Box 236, Swindon, Wiltshire SN3 6QZ

Copyright   ©   Leonard L Bridge(1995)

ISBN   1 872308 77 5

British Library Cataloguing-in-Publication Data. A catalogue record for this
book is available from the British Library.

Printed by: The Da Costa Print and Finishing Company
           35 Queensland Road
           London N7 7AH

ACKNOWLEDGEMENTS

This book would have been only a memory stored in the attic but for the prompting from my friends and family and former RAF colleagues.

Appendix A   Submitted by: Ex-Warrant Officer R S Angell
              No.968942, Flight Engineer Coastal Command
              Royal Air Force.

Appendix B   Submitted by: A Scammells, Ex-Royal Regiment of
              Artillery.

Appendix C   Submitted by: Cpl J Robinson, Ex-Royal Air
              Air Force East Wretham.

Appendix D   Submitted by: Les Bridge, Ex-Royal Air Force
              Newtown.

Appendix E   Submitted by: Albert Thomas, Flt Lt Engineer,
              Bomber Command.

In some instances names of people mentioned in this book have been changed to avoid distress or embarrassment.

CONTENTS

Contents (contined)

LIST OF ILLUSTRATIONS

ABOUT THE AUTHOR

I was the eldest of five born in St. Helens, Lancashire and in 1918 we moved to the picturesque village of Ffestiniog, North Wales. At the age of 14 I won a scholarship to enter the County Grammar School at a distance of three miles from Ffestiniog. Due to the severe depression of the late twenties and early thirties, I, as the eldest boy in the family felt I had a duty to supplement the family income. I was hired as a farm hand with a very able farmer. He had lost his son who had been struck down by lightning in a heavy storm. I felt, after a trial period that farming was a non starter and I resigned, after having obtained a post as a counter assistant in a general grocery store outlet with a very well known stores outlet by the trade name 'Melias', situated in the town of Blaenau Ffestiniog. It was a few months later that I was asked by the travelling district Company General Manager if I would consider extensive training to become a local manager. After a few months I decided that the retail shopping business had little appeal and I decided to resign and in the early part of 1933 I joined the Merchant Navy as cabin boy and later served on deck as ordinary seaman.

In the spring of 1935 I was well advised by a Captain who had two sons in the Royal Air Force to enlist in that service and the reasons have been mentioned in the book.

I heeded his advice and enlisted in the RAF in the autumn of 1935. This period then spanned thirty years. On discharge I took over the tenancy of a 'Regent' petrol and servicing station, a new complex in the so called petrol alley in Park Street - Devizes, Wiltshire. I received two very favourable articles in the Regent Company annual magazine for that period.

I decided to leave the area after a two year period and immediately was on my way to fill an advertised post of 'Chief Technical Clerk' in Westinghouse Brake and Signal Company, based in Chippenham, Wiltshire, a few miles from my home in Devizes.

The post was interesting and rewarding but I decided to move to Newtown in Powys, mid Wales and purchased a livestock and general haulage business. I sold my interest in the business when the time was ripe and set up a Company under the name of Leonard L. Bridge - 'Mid Wales Catering Co. and Contract Furniture', with a modest retail outlet shop in Newtown. At the age of 65 I closed down the Company (after a period of 15 years) and moved into retirement.

I wish to thank my wife, a lady from Finland who supported me in the various stages of the book and also to my eldest son, Dr.John L Bridge, ex University of Bristol, my youngest son, Mike Bridge BSc, ex RAF pilot and now a First Officer pilot in British Airways and a special mention to my youngest son's wife, Marilyn who is an Air Traffic Controller at Heathrow, London, who kindly word processed and brought my book to fruition.

By the KINGS Order the name of
Sergeant L.L.Bridge
Royal Air Force
was published in the London Gazette on
14th January 1944
as mentioned in a Despatch for distinguished service,
I am charged to record
His Majesty's high appreciation

Signed: Archibald Sinclair
Secretary of State for Air.

Copy from the original document as per 14th January 1944.
Re-London Gazette.

INTRODUCTION

I was urged by my former RAF colleagues to write a book under the title of 'An Airman's Lot', a subject that would bring to the fore the strong bond between the gallant 'Air Crew' and the 'Ground Staff'. I did not realise at the time what a daunting task it would turn out to be and after twelve months of concentrated research and effort the book began to take shape. Covering thirty years in the RAF from 1935-1965 one cannot fail to accumulate a considerable amount of knowledge, expertise and above all a close contact with different types of individuals from 'civvy' street, from all walks of life as the saying goes. There were civilians called up from different occupations under the 'National Service' act, in time of war, with minds of their own and they were subjected to the great leveller of service life and discipline.

The heraldic inscription 'Per Ardua Ad Astra' (Through Difficulties To The Stars) and 'Esprit de Corps', which I regarded as 'One for all and all for one', took on a stronger meaning during the Second World War. Morale was also high and did not waver throughout the difficult time ahead.

A close friend of mine, Roy Roberts mentioned in the book, had he survived the war would most probably be a contributor in his memoirs as pilot. We must not forget the role of the 'WAAFS' who played their part in the RAF and as a senior non commissioned officer, when assembling the squadron on parade, one could not help but notice the change in the airmens' turn out. The dreaded F252 - "On a charge form" became almost a relic....I wonder why!

FOREWORD

Air Commodore J C Atkinson CBE

Most air force reminiscences are written by aircrew from the cockpit. The recorded experiences of airmen groundcrew are more rare and Leonard Bridge's account of his Royal Air Force service is welcome on that account alone, but for much else besides. His thirty years in uniform spanned the era of expansion of the Trenchard Air Force in 1935, accelerating to the outbreak of war and the enormous build up of the Service to one and a quarter million, to be followed by the post-war contraction in the national service era, and so back to the all-volunteer RAF that he left in 1965. During this time he served at numerous operational and training stations in the United Kingdom, as well as in Malta, Egypt and Germany.

He records with insight and good humour his experiences during three decades of profound change and challenge, and how they affected him, his close friends and fellow airmen. Service readers will readily related to the account of his training days, whilst his description of life on wartime bomber airfields and later of the post-war troubles in the Suez Canal Zone, with their danger and hardships as well as the lighter side, will evoke many memories amongst those in uniform during these years.

Leonard Bridge brings out clearly the strength of RAF life with its camaraderie and esprit de corps in good times and in bad, which was the common experience of all who served. He also tells us something of his interests; of the history of places where he was posted, of his musical talents and of some of the notable events in which he became involved.

I commend his book to all who served, whether air or groundcrew, and to a wider readership seeking a feel for life in the Royal Air Force from an airman's point of view.

July 1994   Ian Atkinson

DEDICATION

This book is being dedicated to 'Sergeant George Osborne' of the Royal Air Force who was stationed on the Canal Zone in Egypt and was instrumental in saving the life of a colleague from near drowning in that notorious stretch of water, the 'Blue Lagoon', in the Egyptian town of Ismailia. The undercurrents belied the shimmering blue and tranquil surface of the lagoon and it was these treacherous waters which claimed so many lives.

The floating pontoon was anchored a hundred yards from the shore and the occupants were watching the swimmers. Suddenly Sgt Osborne, who was on the pontoon, noted that one of the swimmers was in difficulty. He appeared to be carrying a boy on his shoulders and the next instant there was only the boy on the surface with no sign of the swimmer. An adverse remark made by another SNCO on the pontoon against the swimmer so incensed Sgt Osborne that he dived for the third time and located the drowning airman. In the murky gloom on the bed of the lagoon he saw a patch of white being rapidly covered by silt, and having secured the airman to himself, brought him back to the surface. There was intense activity on the pontoon for the next few minutes which called for mouth to mouth resuscitation. The airman was revived and taken to the RAF hospital suffering from water in the lungs, resulting in the airman, an SNCO, being out of circulation for a while and his medical record annotated a 'Case of near drowning'. It is true that one can see a flashback of one's life in these circumstances, and this, coupled with two other similar incidents, had a traumatic effect on the airman concerned.

AUTHORS NOTE

In the following story, I will attempt to portray the lives of those gallant aircrew and ground staff with whom I was privileged to serve from the early 30s and cover World War II and onwards to my discharge from the RAF in 1965. A special mention will be made of 311 Czech Squadron of No.3 Group, Bomber Command based in East Anglia and those wonderful aircraft the Wellingtons, affectionately called the 'Flying Pigs'. The early warning system of those feathered friends the pheasants, which would cry out in unison in the woods surrounding the aircraft dispersal points at least an hour before any hostile aircraft approached our airfield, did save lives, and was more accurate than the display of coloured flags, where the red would appear as alert, as the bombers were unloading their first stick of bombs overhead.

One of the main characters in the book will be one Clifford Lewis, born in St Helens, Lancashire, the home of the famous Pilkington Glass works, and of the Beechams Pills complex. His father was a Staff/Sgt in the East Lancs Regiment in World War I and was on active service in France when Cliff was born. Three months after his birth he developed a series of convulsions and his family doctor informed his mother that he would not survive the year of his birth. By those quirks of fate, and old wives' tales, his mother was instructed to take the child in the vicinity of the gas works where tar was being used on road resurfacing.

After a few days there was a dramatic change for the better and to this day I understand that there has been no re-occurrence of his complaint. It was in 1922 that his parents decided to move to his mother's birthplace, the picturesque village of Ffestiniog, buried amidst the hills and mountains in North Wales. The inhabitants were a very close community, chapel goers of strict moral standards, but gentle and kind. Due to the real depression of the 30s, a diminishing family income, ever increasing dole queues, and the dreaded means test, Cliff's promising academic career was cut short. Events preceding his entry into the Royal Air Force are mentioned in detail in order that the readers will be able to formulate their own opinions, particularly we, the older generation, on the trials, setbacks and hardships in those grim days of the 30s.

Some of the events are humorous, others extremely sad. Esprit-de-corps in those days in the Armed Forces was of a very high standard. Unfortunately it is not practised today with the same intensity as that of the war years. Airmen of the older generation will recall, and live in part, similar experiences recorded in this book. Inter-unit postings at home and abroad, the uprooting of firmly ensconced old timers in married quarters, and the ingenious ways used by airmen of having their postings cancelled, or deferred on compassionate grounds. I shall not go into the pregnancy factor! The breed of officers in the war years was exceptional but there would be the odd character who would exercise his authority without tact and diplomacy on unfortunate airmen who incurred their wrath. These airmen would thus be unable to extricate themselves from trivial incidents without loss of dignity and wounded pride especially when the F252, the dreaded 'On a charge' form was dismissed by their own senior officer who would take the charge.

The unique ability of one titled officer, we shall call him Lord Danvers, although this was not his real name, who was a pilot under training and held the rank of Pilot Officer. He had the knack of landing Hawker Harts, Furys and Audax biplanes nose in or on their backs on the soft turf of the airfield. There were no runways in those days and on some of the earlier models, the tail wheels culminated into a tail skid, a metal shoe, which assisted in the drag during landings. Two of the humorous landings are depicted in photographs in this book with Lord Danvers 'at the helm' as it were.

The discovery of a lady's body with the leg protruding from the soft earth in the undergrowth of a forest, complete with silken hose and silver coloured shoe, and the amusing sequel when the police were called. Why our Squadron was confined to barracks immediately after the state funeral of our beloved King George V.

The events which followed the overthrow of King Farouk of Egypt and the full scale riots within the Canal Zone, the murder of Sister Theresa and several nuns at Ismailia, women and children and the mutilated bodies of our comrades found floating in the so called Sweet Water canal. The word sweet in this context is somewhat obscure as it was the normal practice if a European was unlucky enough to fall in the canal that he would be rushed to the nearest military hospital for a series of injections.

The hanging of a British soldier in the hills, found guilty of the alleged murder of a taxi driver in Cairo and my encounter with this unsavoury character at the Blue Kettle Club in Ismailia whilst we were entertaining servicemen and their wives in our capacity as members of the Royal Air Force band of El-Firdan.

The arrival of Sir Winston Churchill, Anthony Eden and the President of the United States of America, F D Roosevelt at Malta, prior to their departure for the 'Yalta Conference'.

How one airman refused to service DC4 aircraft of BOAC, his mistaken idea that one senior officer was a shareholder, and his sudden departure from the unit.

My psychic experiences prior to the outbreak of World War II and the strange apparition seen by three airmen and myself at Royal Air Force station Honington preceding a bomber attack on our station.

The beautiful mural paintings depicting scenes of Czechoslovakia in our nissen huts, painted by Czech aircrew, whose daring and courage were never in doubt.

I was privileged to be one of the senior non commissioned officers in charge of 'A' Flight ground crew and for a period of three years worked with these dedicated ground and air crews.

The book concludes with a few anecdotes submitted by former colleagues plus a personal tribute to the Royal Air Force, both officers and airmen.

CHAPTER I

ENLISTMENT INTO THE RAF AT WEST DRAYTON

It was in November 1935 that I decided to apply to enlist in the Royal Air Force. A few days after I'd sent the application, I received a buff coloured envelope with the word OHMS, from the village postman, who remarked in his usual jocular manner, "I bet it is a final demand on an unpaid bill!". As we chatted on the doorstep, I hastily opened the envelope with the postman breathing heavily down my neck. One must take one's hat off to these colourful characters. "I see that you are joining the RAF then, Cliff", and he hastily left, no doubt to pass on the news. The letter was from the recruiting officer in Liverpool.

'You are requested to report on Monday in Liverpool, with your case, and be prepared to stay overnight in the city. You must be at the recruiting centre no later than 0900hrs'.

There were no travel warrants or expenses for the initial interview. I left home on Sunday evening, with the intention of hitch-hiking a distance of 120 miles. After a series of hops on all kinds of mechanical transport plus a small delay on the Ferry crossing from Birkenhead to Liverpool, I arrived at the city centre at approximately 2200hrs. I managed to obtain lodgings (bed and breakfast) not far from the recruiting office for the sum of two shillings and sixpence. I awoke on Monday morning early, and having breakfasted on bangers and mash, no doubt the remains of the Sunday main meal, a mug of strong tea sweetened with condensed milk, and having thanked the landlady, with a promise to stay with the family again on my next visit to Liverpool, I made my way to the recruiting office. I was the first to arrive and was greeted by a young man in blue uniform, with two chevrons on his arm, who introduced himself as Corporal Hewitt. Having taken my particulars, he directed me to a large waiting room, where I was in a position to observe the arrival of other hopeful recruits.

Amongst the candidates was one man in his early thirties, who wasted little time in introducing himself as Jack Jones and who immediately dominated the general conversation, mostly on his achievements as a qualified general engineer and his forthcoming plans to transform the engineering branch of the Royal Air Force. Twenty minutes later, after a non-stop lecture to a subdued and bored audience and due to the arrival of the recruiting officer, we were ushered to the medical section for a physical examination. There were thirty of us altogether. Afterwards, out of the original thirty, twenty of us assembled in the waiting room - the others had been found medically unfit. Jack Jones was with us of course with the comment,"Nothing to it old boy!".

1

At approximately 1100hrs we entered another room for an arithmetic test, an essay on why we wanted to join the RAF and lastly a questionnaire, consisting of 100 questions with yes/no answers. We completed our papers and were told to report back at 1400hrs. We were all assembled in the waiting room when the recruiting officer arrived carrying a sheaf of papers and without further preamble, he proceeded to call out our names. "After each name called, you will receive a number, either No 1 or No 2, and you will wait in the room showing that number on the door". There were twelve of us in room No 1, including Jack Jones and the other eight were in room No 2. The recruiting officer's first words on arrival were,"Congratulations lads, you have passed the initial phase," and it was only at that moment that we realised that room No 1 was the pass room. We then received our instructions, travel warrants and expenses, in my case twelve shillings in all. We were to proceed to our respective homes and await further instructions. We felt very proud and elated, and decided to celebrate our initial victory and invited J.Jones for a drink at the nearest pub. Price of beer from the barrel was fourpence a pint and by the time we had made our way to the station, we were slightly inebriated and the worse for wear.

On the 17th November 1935, the long awaited buff coloured envelope arrived at my home, together with travel documents, a week's pay of twelve shillings, a railway warrant and instructions to report to Royal Air Force West Drayton for trade selection and for signing on as a regular, for a minimum period of twelve years.

I hauled out my battered old suitcase and was ready at 0700hrs to catch the early morning train to Crew for the connection to West Drayton. I made my way to the local station, thirty minutes early to be greeted by the local porter, John Owen. This was the era of the GWR, LMS and the LNER, and in those nostalgic days, one would find a coal fire burning brightly in the clean and well kept waiting rooms and neat wall to wall black leather covered bench seating together with the old 'nestles penny a bar' chocolate machines. The porter would pop his head in to the waiting room to ask if any passenger would care for a hot mug of tea, free of charge.

The station was spotless, with carefully tended plants and flowers, when in season. The signalman was enclosed in the small signal box ready to change the points and the red to green lights and one could watch the steam train arrive, slow and graceful and the engine driver accept a very large key shaped object to be handed into the next station and so on.

These were the good old days when porters would carry the heavy luggage of the elderly and politely refuse to accept tips, a far cry from today's preoccupation with strikes, higher wages, indifferent and lower

2

standards of services. The coach compartments were exceptionally clean, with white linen covered head rests. Railway chiefs and unions please note! It would be revealing to the younger generation if the television networks would dig into their archives and show films of the smooth and efficient running of railways in those heydays of the thirties.

On our arrival at Crewe station, I immediately made for the station restaurant, for the usual cup of tea and slab of bread pudding when I was met by a chorus of greetings by former colleagues from the recruiting office in Liverpool,"Here comes Taffy." Amongst the lads was our friend Jack Jones, and as we awaited the arrival of our connections to the south, we were resigned to a continuation of Jack's series of lectures. The other three lads in the group were Davidson, Richards and Bennet, the latter was later to be dubbed the 'Barrack Room Lawyer'.

We arrived at the railway station of West Drayton at approximately 1800hrs. There was a slight ground frost and at the ticket barrier there was a delay of one hour. Apparently, Davidson had lost his railway warrant and it was only by the intervention of a burly uniformed corporal who had been detailed to meet us that he was allowed to proceed. Outside in the gathering gloom, was the RAF transport, a Bedford, with a canvas tilt, and we were told to hop smartly into the rear of the vehicle. Finally, we were on our way to RAF station West Drayton.

Our first impression of the staton, was a favourable one. At the entrance was a barrier, painted in blue and immediately to the left was the guardroom, manned by the duty service police. Hanging on hooks in a neat row, were firebuckets, painted red and immediately facing us, was a small reception hatch. The burly corporal reported in, with a nominal roll of all the new arrivals and with these formalities over, we were directed to our barrack room. Ours was No 6, a wooden type of barracks, situated in rows of a neat and tidy complex. There were well trimmed lawns surrounding each 'hut' as we called them. The interior of each hut was lined with a thick highly polished brown linoleum floor covering, and in the centre of the room was a cast iron cylindrical stove, with a stack pipe leading out through the roof, and complemented by a coal scuttle.

There were twenty four cast iron beds, twelve in a row, head to toe on either side. The palliasses or matresses were made of good quality straw, and neatly stacked was the bolster pillow, on grey woollen blankets, three in number, the regulation maximum. There were slim lined wooden lockers to each bed space for the personal use of the occupant for their belongings. We were busy unpacking and settling in, when, framed in the doorway was an airman, with two propeller badges on his arms. "Stand by your beds, you shower of twits!", and he wasted no time in bringing us to heel. This little episode brought us to the grim reality of the commencement of service life and what we had undertaken. "My name is Chapman, Leading Aircraftsman Chapman. I am in charge of you lot and you will stand to attention when I wish to speak to you at all times." This gentleman was a self opinionated egoistical and vindictive character. For reasons known only to himself he selected Jones and myself for fatigues. Having noted our names, and bed space allocations, he would bawl out with a voice that would do credit to Sgt Major Brittain. He would delegate barrack room duties, for which the primary aim was to cater for the well being of one certain Chapman.

At one end of the room was a wooden partitioned bunk, the domain of our mentor. "You there Jones, will bring me a hot mug of tea from the adjoining cookhouse at 0600hrs sharp. You Lewis will make up my bed daily and you Davidson will press my uniform and polish my boots until your face is mirrored in the toe caps."

Our stay at West Drayton was to be for a period of fourteen days and we would be interviewed by specialists both service and civilian for training within the trade group that we had applied for at Liverpool recruiting office. There were several rooms fitted out with the equipment applicable to each trade, wireless sets, aircraft components, armaments, general engineering items and so forth. I proceeded to the wireless section, as I had high hopes for a career as a wireless operator. There was in attendance the examining officer, and a civilian sitting quietly in the corner of the room. I later found out that he was known as trick-cyclist, the nick name given to the psychologist. Questions asked varied from any knowledge of wireless and associated equipment to pertinent questions on my social background, family and previous employment.

Unfortunately I was not accepted for this particular trade, but instead was recommended for intensive training as Flight Rigger, commencing as AC2, ie aircraftsman second class, with the trade of fitters mate, which would eventually lead to the flight riggers' course and a higher trade group.

We were on standby in our billet, when in stormed Jones. Without a word of greeting he commenced to pack his personal kit and at that moment our friend Chapman appeared and bellowed to Jones, "You there, on the double and bring me an extra blanket from the stores!". Jones turned around facing Chapman and said in an unusually quiet voice, "Are you talking to me little man? You can get stuffed Chapman and get your own bloody blanket and further more we do not have to stand to attention to the likes of you. This applies to officers and senior non commissioned officers only. Any further truck from you my boy and I shall assist you to vacate the billet with the weight of my shoe to your rear. A word of advice to you lads, you are not bound to see to the

4

welfare of LAC Chapman, but rather the reverse and the official sharing of barrack room duties only".

In the stunned silence that ensued Chapman made a hasty retreat and rushed out of the billet in double time, no doubt to recover his dignity.

It transpired that Jones had failed to make direct entry into the engineering branch of the Royal Air Force and had declined to enlist in a lower grade. It was with a degree of respect that we bade Jones farewell and wished him continued success in civvy street.

The next day a chastened Chapman entered our billet and instructed us to report to the 'Administration' wing for the taking of the Oath of Allegiance to the Crown. We were now confirmed as enlisted men on a twelve year engagement.

On the Friday we were briefed for our next move or posting and were supplied with the movement order and travel warrants. The rest of the week was a memorable one at West Drayton and except for a few light station duty fatigues we were otherwise free to explore the town. Our trip included a visit to the 16th century gateway from a former manor house, a critical look at the few Georgian houses, the old church with the 15th century font, the very fine monuments and a notable chalice and paten of 1507.

Monday arrived and I had the additional responsibility of being airman in charge of the party.

We were to report to Royal Air Force Uxbridge for kitting up and intensive training in arms drill, ceremonial parades, obedience and the merging of ones identity to the common cause.

CHAPTER II

SQUARE BASHING, RAF UXBRIDGE

We arrived at Royal Air Force station Uxbridge within a few hours having been picked up by service transport. The town of Uxbridge, in the county of Middlesex lies on the river Colne and the Grand Junction Canal. St. Margaret's church dates back to the 14th and 15th century, the tower having been rebuilt in 1820. The Old Treaty House was certainly the worse for wear and the famous 'George Inn' was reputed to have associations with the meeting of Charles I and Parliament in 1645. There was also a most interesting Market House dating from 1789.

Our first impression of the RAF station was of a miniature town, well lit by rows of lamp standards, with trim lawns, solid brick barrack blocks and red gravel paths with the blocks named after famous personalities. There were both military and foreign names relating to incidents of a historical nature. Entrance to the camp was through blue painted barriers and in the foreground was the Guardroom, painted in a vivid green. Hanging on hooks on the outside wall were a few fire buckets, painted in red with the words FIRE stencilled in black, containing either sand or water. The guardroom was manned by a sergeant, a corporal and one airman of the service police, the latter wore an armband with the letters SP for service police.

Having ascertained our particulars, we were directed to our living quarters and were relieved to discover that our party would be housed together at Arras Block on the second floor of the three storey block. The barrack room overlooked a massive square which we learned later was the sacred parade ground and was dominated by the RAF flag, flying high and proudly on a white flag pole.

The barrack room was huge in comparison to our previous billet, with a large bed space for each occupant. The iron beds were in two neat rows head to toe from the opposing walls. These were sprung and not with the usual lattice metal bracings that we were accustomed to. The heating came from a central boiler, which supplied central heating to the various blocks and was coal and coke fired. The ablutions adjoined each floor, with a number of showers, baths, and hand basins. The floors had the usual heavy plain, highly polished brown linoleum. Next to each bed head was a steel locker to be strictly used for service kit and uniforms only. All items of civilian gear were delegated to our suitcases in the adjoining storeroom well out of sight. We were relieved to find that our blankets, sheets and pillows were already allocated and stacked neatly at the bed head. At one end of the room was a large black notice board on which was prominently displayed Station Standing Orders

(SSOs) - Personnel Occurence Reports (PORs), Daily Routine Orders (DROs) and a blank weekly roster of barrack room duties.

There were thirty recruits per floor in each of the three storey barrack blocks and a regular general duty corporal was in charge of each floor. Our junior NCO was called Corporal Richards, a dedicated serviceman who apparently was to be our guiding light for the duration of our stay at the camp.

"Stand by your beds' he bawled out to us recruits, 'And make it snappy, I haven't got all day to waste on you lot." In his hands he held a thin black board, to which was clipped a foolscap sheet of paper. "You there," he shouted to the recruit nearest to him, "what is your name, rank and number?" This particular recruit who had been introduced to us previously was called AC2 Bennet, with the reputation of being a barrack room lawyer and the following dialogue ensued. "My name happens to be Bennet guv." The corporal turned a shade of white and remarked in a controlled voice, "Come here boy and stand to attention to an NCO. What is your name?"...."My name is Bennet." "What comes after Bennet and what are these stripes on my arm?" By this time we were all smiles, which did not go unnoticed by the corporal.

Having taken the nominal roll of all the occupants, the corporal handed out to each of us our personal identification bed card and we were told to fill in the necessary particualrs, namely, name, rank, number and religion and to slot the said cards into the holders directly above our bed heads. The corporal then remarked, "As the night is young, immediately you have settled in, you will carry out the barrack room duties shown on the fatigue roster posted up on the notice board." We were then detailed to polish the floor and dust and polish the windows, although it was dark outside. "You there Bennet will polish the linoleum. You will find you polishing bumpers and felt pads in the broom cupboard on the landing. I shall be back here at 2130hrs and you will stand by your beds for my inspection." With a gleam in his eye, and a wave to Bennet, he was off. Somehow we had the vague impression that our corporal had a slight streak of malice in his character and that we would have to be more careful in future.

At 2130hrs the corporal turned up to inspect his patch as he termed it, and except for a few minor faults, he seemed to be perfectly satisfied with the general turn out, no doubt mellowed by a flagon of beer.
Immediately after his inspection, we were then briefed on the following day's events. "Reveille will be at 0630, breakfast at 0700 and the dining hall will be vacated by 0730. You will all report back here and will report to the station barber for short back and sides. After lunch you will report to the general clothing stores for kitting up and then to the armoury for your rifles and bayonets. You will all assemble in the

barrack room at 1600 sharp."

That evening we retired at 2230 as we had no other option, due to LIGHTS OUT, a feat accomplished by our corporal, by turning off the main switch.

In the early hours of the morning, we were awakened by the station bugler, playing 'Reveille', followed by a menacing figure in the doorway. This character who later transpired to be the orderly sergeant wore a blue webbing belt around his ample waist and on his right arm, a band with the letters OS (Orderly Sergeant). The figure advanced, tipping out the recruits with the words, "Wakey wakey, you shower of twits." By the time he had reached my bed I was up and partly dressed.

On completion of ablutions, there would be a rush to the dining room with the sole purpose of being first in the queue. Our first impression of the dining room was favourable. There were rows of wooden tables with polished tops, and bench seats. Standing at the servery were the airmen of the general duties branch in white coats and in front of them were large roasting tins, filled with fried eggs and bacon. One very large pan contained porridge. Stacked neatly were metal three division containers, into which was ladled a portion of porridge in one division and egg and bacon in the others. To complete the fare, were two thick slices of bread, a pat of margarine, and a mug of strong tea. Breakfast fares alternated between kippers, bubble and squeak (a mixture of mashed potatoes, cabbage, and corned beef) and of course the top favourite egg and bacon, which was served twice weekly.

One amusing incident occurred when we were served bubble and squeak. The orderly officer arrived in the dining room accompanied by the orderly sergeant. The latter bawled out as follows: "Attention for the Orderly Officer. Any complaints?" We then sat back to see who would complain. In this particular instance our colleague dared to voice a complaint. "Yes,sir," he remarked, "There is a slug in my bubble and squeak." The orderly sergeant carefully removed the slug, and handing it to Bennet he remarked, "Hand it over to the cook and he will be only too pleased to re-cook it for your lunch."

Sunday tea time was the worst meal of the week. This would consist of bread and jam, followed by a thick slice of dundee cake. We would quickly devour this meagre fare and quietly move to the next floor for a repeat. Unfortunately, and by coincidence, Bennet was recognised by the same orderly sergeant, who happened to be on duty and must have observed Bennet on the first floor. The orderly sergeant approached and in a quiet voice, spoke to Bennet, "You were on the first floor just now so I shall now place you on a charge," and he produced a F252, a charge form, which was to be a familiar document in the weeks ahead. The orderly sergeant failed to recognise the remainder of us on the table.

Whilst the orderly sergeant was taking down Bennet's particulars, I whispered to one of our colleagues that I intended to support Bennet. I turned to the sergeant and said, "I am also guilty." The remainder of our colleagues followed suit.

The total charges were fifteen. This episode was a field day for the sergeant, with an eye to promotion to flight sergeant. This supporting act on Bennet's behalf, was the beginning of esprit-de-corps which was to prove invaluable in the turbulent years ahead. Later we were ushered with caps off into the augustus presence of a squadron leader of the administration branch, by the gleeful sergeant, who shouted commands of "Left, right, left, right, attention!"

Having read out the charge of, in effect stealing rations, by consuming second helpings on a different floor of the dining room, and taking into account that we volunteered to support Bennet, there was a long pause. We were then marched out, to await individual sentences. A few minutes later we were marched back. The squadron leader was impressed with our turn out in best blue, with our pantaloons pressed, our putees at the correct height and the toe caps of our ankle boots shining with the special effort we had made to create the maximum impression. We had a lecture on the seriousness of consuming unauthorised rations and to our surprise, the case was dismissed.

Outside in the corridor, the sergeant passed us and muttered, "There is no justice." The squadron leader was of the old school and nearing retirement, with years of experience and this kindly gesture on his part, proved to be a salutary lesson to us all at the beginning of our career.

A couple of weeks later we noticed a considerable improvement in Sunday teas, with a hot meal provided.

After our first breakfast at the station, we made our way to the station barber, for short back and sides. After lunch we were assembled outside the clothing stores and were ushered into the presence of a flight sergeant, who was directing the activities of two airmen and the camp tailor in the issue of uniforms and sundries. Our best blue or No. 1 uniform consisted of pantaloons, putees, topcoat, ceremonial hat, webbing, underclothing, overalls, or denims, and a kitbag. From there we proceeded to the station armoury for our rifles and bayonets. The webbing previously issued at the clothing stores, consisted of cross straps, ammunition pouches, a pack which would be carried on our backs and a ceremonial webbing belt.

We were in our billet promptly by 1600hrs with Cpl Richards in attendance accompanied by a sergeant and a flight sergeant. These latter SNCOs were to be our drill instructors. They introduced themselves as F.Sgt Danvers and Sgt Robinson. We were ordered to report and assemble on the square at 0830hrs and we were briefed on what items of clothing to wear.

Promptly at 0830hrs we assembled on the square and after the roll call we were split into squads, lettered A-J, each squad consisting of 48 recruits. I was allocated to 'A' squad. The senior drill instructor, F.Sgt Danvers was standing to attention, dressed in pantaloons, putees, his ceremonial hat square, the shiny peak low over his eyes. His polished buttons of his overcoat and buckles of his ceremonial belt around his waist glinted in the rays of the rising sun. Under his arm was crooked a short black ebony stick with a silver top. The sergeant carried a gadget which we later recognised as a metronome, this useful instrument was called a pacer. The first few weeks involved a gruelling eight hours square bashing, as we called practising marching in fours, and learning strict obedience and high standards of discipline.

Later we were to visit the rifle range for target practice and on our first day there were a few bruises, due to the failure of holding the rifle firmly to the shoulder when firing. The recoil of the rifle would be felt on the shoulder as a dull thud. The pass mark on targets was above average and we all received marks over the magic norm of 60% and some of us obtained 80%.

We were coming to the end of our square bashing days and our squad became highly proficient in arms drill and ceremonial parades. We were now well into the year of 1936 when news was received of the passing of our beloved sovereign King George V. Consequently our postings were deferred and we were selected to represent Royal Air Force Uxbridge and to line the Mall for the State Funeral.

The day arrived when we were loaded into Bedford QL tilt covered trucks and arrived at the Mall three hours prior to the sad ceremony due to take place. Having taken our place on the route, we were ordered to present on your arms reverse. In this position we were able to squint at the oncoming cortege.

Preceding the gun carriage conveying the body of our King, were the mass bands with their drums muffled in black material. Behind the gun carriage were the members of our Royal Family and immediately behind, European Kings and Queens, followed by the Heads of State of the Commonwealth countries, members of the Government and representatives of the Armed Services. One incident worthy of note related to our particular contingent. When the cortege had passed, AC2 Bennet keeled over and dropped his rifle. F.Sgt Danvers, our drill flight sergeant became extremely agitated and in a controlled voice said to Bennet,"Pick up that bloody rifle, Bennet." To drop one's rifle on a ceremonial occasion was unthinkable and a poor reflection on oneself. On our return to barracks we stood to attention to F.Sgt Danvers and all hell was let loose. "Bennet!", he remarked,"Give me your rifle," and on receipt he flung the said rifle through the window. It landed on the square amidst a shower of glass. "Bennet!", he shouted,"Retrieve that rifle at the double." On his return the flight sergeant, who had completely lost his cool remarked in a loud voice that there would be a collective barrack room charge on damages to the window and that there would be deductions from pay. This was not the end of the incident and we all received an extra week in arms drill until we could manipulate the rifles with the dexterity of a conjurer.

Our experiences at Royal Air Force Uxbridge created a deep and lasting impression upon us and as a gesture to our drill flight sergeant we decided to lash out as it were and purchased a silver cigarette lighter with the following inscription: *FROM THE LADS OF 'A' SQUADRON, TO F.Sgt Anvers.*

We duly presented the lighter and the poor chap was overcome with emotion. A few days later our postings came through. Bennet was posted to a wireless operators' school, Davidson to 'armament', Richardson to 'equipment' and myself to Royal Air Force Henlow, dubbed the 'Pickle Factory.' This nickname was obscure to me at the time. I was to attend a nine month's Flight Riggers' Course, a step up from fitter's mate.

Our postings were effective from the Monday and we had the weekend to have a binge at the local pub.

This was to be the last get together of our squad and in later years I heard over the grapevine, during World War II that Bennet and Davidson, having remustered to Air Crew, were killed over Germany. On the Monday morning, prior to departure for our various destinations, we received our mail. One interesting letter was from my friend Roy, from RAF Halton, informing me that he had been selected for aircrew and would be training for pilot, at home and abroad. This news left me depressed as I had a vivid flash back to the dream involving Roy. I immediately phoned Halton and was put in touch with Roy and I tried to persuade him not to accept the remustering, but my efforts were to no avail.

Later I thought perhaps it was my imagination that was at fault. Here we are in the year of 1937 with no hint of the holocaust to come and yet I had that uneasy feeling of a terrible human tragedy, involving the whole of mankind. On our way to the station, I was unusually quiet. The remark from one of my comrades,"Cheer up taff, you look like death warmed up!", did not help.

We parted company for our various destinations and I settled down to the rail journey to Henlow.

11

CHAPTER III

FLIGHT RIGGERS COURSE, RAF HENLOW

I arrived at the railway terminus of Hitchin and on the platform were several airmen, their destination was Royal Air Force Henlow. I did not know any of them but this was short lived and there were introductions all round. Such was the bond and comradeship in those days.

The drivers of the service transport informed us that there would be a two hour delay to transport us on the seven mile journey to Henlow, as there would be other new arrivals due on later trains.

Six of us decided to explore the town. Hitchin in Hertfordshire has a large Perp. church incorporating a fine porch and excellent screenwork. There are a number of old houses, particularly in Tilehouse and Bridge street. Here one can see the 'Coopers Arms' and 'Sun Inn' and also the 'Biggin' almhouses. Hitchin Priory, dating from 1770 contains fragments of a 14th century carmelite house and retains its moat. The Skynner almhouses in Bancroft date from 1670 and 1698. The town was the birthplace of George Chapman, the poet and there are also associations with Lord Lytton's 'Eygene Aram'. Six miles west are the wooded Barton hills with the prehistoric hill fort of Ravensburgh Castle. London was only 34.5 miles from Hitchin, with Luton a mere 8.25 miles. Hitchin was to be our base on our time off.

We decided to have a meal at the YMCA, which consisted of a round of fried bread, two sausages, beans and fried egg and a mug of strong tea. From here a quick visit to the nearest pub for a pint of ale. The meal came to ninepence each and the beer to fourpence a pint. We then hared back to the station with only minutes to spare and were bundled into the waiting truck by a burly sergeant with a minimum of ceremony and with the following words ringing in our ears, "I shall have your guts for garters you shower of twits." We had failed to notify the sergeant that we were visiting the town and he had already crossed our names off the nominal roll as having not turned up. Ah well, live and learn!

RAF Henlow...Bedfordshire - 5 miles NW of Hitchin.

The role of RAF Henlow was under pressure during the 1935 RAF Expansion Scheme, there was considerable demand upon the Ground Technician Provision and the Home Aircraft Depot became an airframe riggers' school. No. 1 Wing trained machine tool operators and fitters No. 3 Wing trained the flight riggers and flight mechanics. By 1938 Henlow's pupil population had reached approximately 5000 and Henlow had forsaken its aircraft repair role. The Parachute Test Unit however remained.

My first impression of RAF Henlow was rows of nissen huts, a large airfied with few hangars. We were allocated quarters in a nissen hut with the same basic layout to that at RAF West Drayton. From the five airmen that I had met at the station at Hitchin, three of them and myself became close friends, which lasted up until the outbreak of war in 1939. There was McGregor, a dour Scotsman from Paisley, a farmer's son, Prescott, the son of a businessman from Leeds and O'Hara from Belfast, the son of a fisherman. This completed the gang of four.

Next morning, having drawn a tool kit and overalls, we reported to the 'Pickle Factory' for the first phase of our technical training, covering a three month course on familiarisation of tools, basic engineering, filing, rivetting, brazing, soldering, physical and mechanical properties of metals, anti-corrosive treatments of metals etc. All this under the eagle eyes of the service and civilian instructors. Standards were of a high and exacting nature, with practical phase exainations, orals and finals. The pass mark was in the region of 60% and we decided to exceed this. Anyone failing to attain the minimum pass mark would be flung off the course and remustered to either ACH - Aircraft Hand or to the GD-General Duty branch. The 'Pickle Factory' was used to eradicate any pre-conceived notions and traces of any civilian skills which did not fit into service thinking. On completion of the basic training, and having qualified, the next and final phase would be the flight riggers' course (airframes) which would last over a six month period.

Physical training was very active at this unit and some days we would be in the gymnasium carrying out what we called physical jerks, including throwing and catching a twelve inch diameter leather ball. As we threw this ball around it seemed to become heavier and heavier and we wondered whether it was lead lined. This particular instrument of torture was called the medicine ball and was the favourite in constant use by an over enthusiastic PT instructor. It was supposed to tone up the muscles, etc.

Outdoor sports consisted of football, rugby and cross country running. I chose football, which later proved to be a total disaster on my part, having scored two goals against my own side and promptly thrown out of the team. O'Hara and Prescott fared no better. They elected to go on the cross country running team, which involved an eight mile run. Twenty of them lined up and they were off. It was a misty day and cold and the course had been mapped out with markers at intervals. There were no check points and apparently, four miles out, O'Hara and Prescott were lost so they decided to return to base at a steady trot. Within sight of the starting point my two mates broke into a gallop and were greeted by the sports officer and onlookers with the words, "Well done lads, you have broken the record." They were presented with their trophies and it was a few minutes later that the red faced airmen told the officer that they had lost their way and had decided to return to base. In the ensuing silence the officer quickly retrieved the trophies, issued a good telling off and dismissed them to their quarters amidst the laughter of the onlookers. With our combined failures in the field of sport, we decided to plump for the medicine ball in the gym.

We were half way through our basic training and averaging 75-82%. With these kinds of marks we decided at the weekend to visit Hitchin and to chat up the local talent and what better than the weekly dance held in the town hall. After a hot meal and a couple of pints in one of the pubs, we wandered over to the town hall. On the stage was a six piece band, pianist, double sax, trumpeter, trombonist and the double base. A dance was in progress to the strain of Blue Moon. We quickly found four partners who were sitting alone in one corner of the room. We made good progress and were looking forward to walking them home towards the end of the session when four men walked in. They approached us and with a wink and a nod one of the men turned to the girls and said, "Time for home my lovelies," and thanked us for entertaining their wives.

We are now in the middle of April 1937 and on our final examinations to complete the first phase of our training. I was relieved when the results came through with above average marks.

On the Monday we reported in to the hangar section for the commencement of the 'Flight Riggers' course. The hangars housed bi-planes on trestles in various stages of assembly. These were the Hawker Harts, the Fury and the Audax. The fuselages and wings were covered in Irish linen and finished off with coats of cellulose dope, a tautening paint with the top coat in the traditional yellow. The wings were separated by struts and braced with adjustable drag and anti drag wires which when adjusted would determine the angle of the main planes to the horizontal and checked by a 3" spirit level in degrees. The water cooled engines were mounted forward and centrally of the cockpit. The landing gears were of the fixed design with a tail skid at the rear. Some of the aircraft had two cockpits which were exposed to the elements. The rear cockpit housed the gunner, and the pilot and the gunner would sit back to back.

Our course consisted of complete assembly of the aircraft mentioned, fabric repairs, cable splicing and so forth.

We were now mid-way through our course, and on the weekend we decided to go scrumaging for apples at a nearby orchard. O'Hara, McGregor, Prescott and myself set forth armed with bolster slips from our pillows. We were previously informed that the farmer who owned the orchard was well disposed towards the services and provided that we

14

picked only the apples that were scattered on the ground we were welcome to indulge. We clambered over the fence and were approximately in the centre of the field leading to the orchard, when all hell was let loose. We had failed to notice the presence of the farmer's prize bull. The first intimation we received, was of the animal pawing the ground, nostrils flared, head lowered and the pointed horns on his head looking ominous. As the stupid animal galloped in our direction we felt that this was our cue to beat a hasty retreat so ran the few yards to the comparative safety of the orchard and the undergrowth. The speed with which we shinned up the trees, if witnessed by the physical training officer, would I am sure, have resulted in an award for the fastest climbers in the world of sport. We were stuck up that tree for at least two hours and were relieved to see that the bull's interest was focused on a few cows that had suddenly appeared from nowhere.

From the vantage point in the tree we could see the surrounding countryside and from the undergrowth we saw what appeared to be a lady's leg protruding from the soft earth, complete with silken hose and a silver shoe. We dared not approach closer, in case the bull would change its mind and we fled from the field. We decided to call the police and dialed 999 at the nearest phone box, a few yards away. Within minutes a black morris car arrived with two police officers.

Out came the little black book and the senior of the two officers, a sergeant, slowly took down the particulars of the incident as we saw it. The senior officer bade us to remain with him whilst the younger officer investigated. We warned him of the bull and he eventually disappeared into the undergrowth. It seemed hours before the young officer returned, his uniform the worse for wear and full of prickly spines. His face was red and we expected him to mention the word murder, but instead he uttered one word - Dummy!. The sergeant gave us a searching look and wondered whether we were taking the mickey out of the police force. He then turned nasty and asked for our service particulars and said that we would be reported for trespassing. I immediately pointed out to the sergeant that general permission had been given by the farmer. We were bundled into the saloon and driven off to see the farmer in order to verify our statement. The farmer was most co-operative and also explained that his children may have buried the dummy as they did have one. The eldest child was summoned and he confessed that they had planted the dummy in that gruesome position and in effect planned the sequel which subsequently occurred. The sergeant muttered about wasting police time and we received a ticking off.

This was the last time that we took advantage of the farmer's kindness, not knowing what his devious and inventive kids would be up to next time around. We settled down to the remainder of the course and in October of the year 1937 we awaited the results of our final oral, practical and written exams. Of our gang of four, Prescott and McGregor received 82% and were earmarked for a group 1 classification, metal riggers' course at RAF Manston. O'Hara received 65% and was posted to North Wales and myself with 78% was posted to RAF Abbotsinch in Scotland.

One alleged incident which occured at RAF Henlow and worthy of a mention was the attendance to witness the drumming out of the service of a sergeant found guilty of theft by a district court martial.

A squadron paraded in best blue as it were and formed a square. Presently the sergeant was marched to the centre of the square, accompanied by a guard. He was bare headed, his ceremonial cap having been removed prior to coming on parade. His stripes were held on his arms by a couple of threads only and the brass buttons on his tunic were attached likewise. An officer approached the sergeant, carrying a sword and when the charge had been read out and the confirmation of the sentence imposed by the court martial, he proceeded to remove the stripes and buttons, by sharp cuts of the sword. The sergeant was then marched from the parade ground. He was no longer in the service and had been discharged with ignominy.

This public disgrace was a deterrent and a warning to anyone who contravened Kings Rules and Air Council Instructions to this extent.

CHAPTER IV

POSTING TO RAF ABBOTSINCH, STRATHCLYDE

RAF Abbotsinch....Strathclyde, Glasgow's fine airport, accommodated the newly formed RAF station HQ on July 1st, under the 6th Auxiliary Group Bomber Command and housed No 602 (City of Glasgow) Fighter Squadron Royal Auxiliary Air Force. They had by now had been re-equipped with Hawker Hinds. Other Hind squadrons included Nos 21 and 34.

No 16 Reconnaissance Group Coastal Command took over the station on January 1st 1937 when 269 squadron was posted in from Bircham Newton with inshore patrols of Avro Ansons. 602 Auxiliary Squadron remained here with both 21 and 34 Squadrons and together with 603 Squadron made a mass fly past over Ibrox stadium on the official opening of the Empire Exhibition by his Majesty the King on May 2nd 1938.

Royal Air Force Abbotsinch, my first operational squadron, proved to be a most rewarding posting and the practical experience I gained proved to be invaluable in later years.

As a flight rigger, my pay had gone up to 26 shillings a week and I was in a position to purchase a second hand motor cycle for the sum of five pounds. This particular contraption was a 250cc twin cylinder Matchless machine. I had purchased it from an airman called Solley, a jewish lad, but after a few weeks I attempted to sell it back to him. It transpired that the cylinders would never work as twins, and would change over cylinders when the going was tough. Solley would not take back the machine under any circumstances, so I was lumbered with it.

RAF Abbotsinch housed No 602 (City of Glasgow) Fighter Squadron, Royal Auxiliary Air Force. The line up of their aircraft was impressive. As the two photographs show.

I was attached to No 269 Squadron, on Avro Ansons. My brief stay at this station produced two incidents worthy of note. I fell foul of a warrant officer - we shall call him W.O. Haynes, who was appointed as technical officer. He was an overweight, bombastic type of character, full of his own importance. During night flying one of the Ansons made a very bad landing. Damage was extensive, but the pilot was unhurt. As I was the senior airman in charge of that aircraft, I mustered up the crash crew to remove it as quickly as possible from the airfield. It had crashed at the end of the airstrip. In those days, the windsock showed the direction of the wind and the landing strip was lit up by two rows of flares, consisting of lamps similar to those of the famous Aladdin. Issuing from the spout was a strip forming a wick and these were fuelled

17

by paraffin. When lit they would light up the landing strip for the aircraft to land. If a crash occurred on the landing strip, the lamps would have to be moved to a new location not windward which would make landing more difficult in an emergency. To save time in trying to locate the warrant officer to obtain permission to move the aircraft, I took full responsibility for the removal. We hastily brought out the crash gear and with the use of two low pressure rubber air bags, which we positioned under the root ends of both wings, and the use of rubber wheeled bogeys, a term used for a short trailer, the aircraft was lifted by air pressure onto the front and rear bogeys, and was quickly towed away. The flare path was then restored to its former location windward.

The following morning I was told to report to W.O. Haynes to receive the biggest rollicking of my service career. The warrant officer had lost all control and shouted in true blue barrack room jargon. "I am the technical officer here, and you are on a charge!". This was followed by several more oaths and references to a doubtful parentage. I was then dismissed for the time being.

A week later my charge came up and I was wheeled infront of a flight commander of the administration branch, a squadron leader. "Although I do not condone a disregard of orders as laid down, I applaud your initiative in clearing the landing strip," and with this comment he dismissed the case. With a sense of relief I left. If I had received a sentence it would have resulted either in being confined to barracks, fatigues, or loss of privileges, plus a record.

The second incident related to a modification to the Avro Anson. On the earlier models it was necessary to remove a large body panel, secured by quick release spring loaded zus slotted screws, to expose a schrader valve to pump up the brakes. I handed the warrant officer a sketch of a small hinged panel secured by one zus screw only, directly over the schrader valve. Although I could not prove it, a replacement Avro Anson did have an identical panel incorporated as per my sketch. I then turned to the warrant officer and said,"Sir, I see that they have modified the panel." The warrant officer smiled and remarked, "Any more bright ideas Lewis pass them on to me!"

602 Auxiliary Squadron Hawker Aircraft line-up. RAF Abbotsinch, Strathclyde, 1938/39

Avro Anson, 269 Squadron, RAF Abbotsinch, 1938/39. LAC Campbell and LAC Allen, Service Crew

Fairey Hendon on display, RAF Abbotsinch, 1938/39

Crashed Hawker aircraft, No.8 FTS. RAF Montrose Angus, 1939/40

Celebrating 100th Faun Refuellers, turn out from AD Struvers, Hamburg. L-R: Herr Grubber, Sgt Lewis, Designer, Herr Goetz. 1952/53

CHAPTER V

No 8 FTS ROYAL AIR FORCE MONTROSE

It was in the autumn of 1938 that I was called in to the orderly room to be informed that I was to be posted to RAF Montrose to NO 8 FTS (Flying Training School). The posting was immediate and was issued with the necessary travel documents and travel warrant. My own transport, the motor cycle had been disposed of through an organised raffle, which had realised six pounds, and with this modest profit, I was more than satisfied.

RAF Montrose...Tayside is the oldest military airfield in Scotland, dating back to 1912, this site is reputed to be steeped in aeronautical history. The airfield was abandoned after the 1st World War but the RAF expansion scheme of 1935 resulted in its activation and consequently the site was purchased for a sum exceeding £18,000.

In 1936 No 8 FTS was formed to train officers and airmen pupils, the aim being to give three months ab-initio flying to each course of 48 trainees, followed by a further three months of intensive advanced training by which time they would qualify to join RAF Squadrons as qualified service pilots.

Hawker Harts and Audaxs were being delivered to the school but aircraft movements were restricted due to the poor surface of the airfield, which required re-turfing and levelling.

The bi-planes were still being operated when the war started but began to be replaced by Master aircraft in May 1940.

The Ansons of 269 Squadron were based between August 25 and October 1939, which we believe was part of the Admiralty plan to concentrate all available aircraft to guard the east coast and to prevent enemy surface raiders breaking into the Atlantic undetected.

The main Coastal Command effort was to form a barrier to ships getting round the north of Scotland from the north German ports.

Montrose was a small town and the Royal Air Force station on the outskirts was surrounded on one side by golden sand dunes, the famous Montrose Basin, and the beautiful Lunan Bay. This posting proved to be one of the best in Scotland, and I resolved to make good use of the golden beach in the summer months ahead.

On arrival at the RAF station, I was to report to the technical officer, a flying officer of the old school and an ex-ranker. This gentleman was strict, and had the knack of inspiring confidence in his subordinates. His technical skills were beyond question and as an ex-ranker he knew all the dodges and angles. God help the unfortunate airman who would try to flannel his way out of an awkward situation. We shall call this officer

Fg Off Riddel. After a few weeks I was called in to his office and was greeted with the following. "I am very pleased with your progress here and I intend to recommend that you proceed to RAF Manston for a self remustering course as Metal Rigger." This was the coveted Group 1 trade with a rise in pay. Continuing the discussion, he added, "You will have to study hard in the next three months, and we will of course give you all our assistance and use of the engineering workshops in your spare time. I advise you to swot hard on a syllabus, closely allied to that given at Manston to those who were on the course. If you pass the examination, without going through the course, it will be a feather in your cap."

The day arrived to go to RAF Manston for the examination and after exhaustive and thorough tests, I was called in to the chief examining officer's office and given the glad news that I had passed with flying colours, having obtained 87%. I was immediately promoted to LAC (Leading Aircraftsman) in the trade of metal rigger. This gave me a slight edge on my comrades.

I was now able to concentrate on my normal duties and one amusing incident occurred. Posted to the unit was a titled officer, under training as pilot officer, we will call him Lord Danvers. He was a good pilot when airborne but his landings were atrocious.

On practice landings and take offs, known as circuits and bumps, the latter phrase can be taken literally as such, he would invariably land his aircraft with the tail pointing proudly to the sky, or the aircraft on its back. After his third mishap, he would have his leg pulled by his co-pilots and many a ribald and uncomplimentary remark, such as 'The upside down pilot', was made.

On his third such landing he would extricate himself from the wrecked plane and report as follows to flying control:-
"I say old chap, the aircraft behaved badly today, it insisted in landing on its back for a change. I have left the damned thing on the edge of the airfield."

On the social side I became friendly with the drum major and was introduced to his family who lived in Montrose and to his very attractive blond sister. His father managed an off licence and his mother was a practising medium. One particular weekend I was invited to a seance in her home and I had permission to bring along a mate of mine who was also inclined towards the occult. A few days prior to the session, my mate had a telegram informing him that his brother had been killed in a motor cycle accident. His brother's name was Dean. We arrived at the home of my friend to be greeted by Mrs Campbell, the mother and taken into the sitting room. We were seated at a circular polished oak table

20

and the only light emanated from a red bulb in a wall bracket holder. In the eerie glow we watched Mrs Campbell who began to breathe heavily, her eyes were closed, and a gold crucifix held in her open palm was visible to all around that table. Whilst concentrating our gaze on the crucifix, the room became very cold and to our amazement, the crucifix faded and it was gone. By this time my friend had become very uneasy but suddenly Mrs Campbell spoke in a deep masculine voice and said. 'I have a message. "This is Dane," not pronounced as Dean, but the next word uttered brought my friend up with a jerk. "This is Yip," a nickname known only to his brother. "I am alive but confused." He described how after the motor cycle accident he was outside his body and gazing at his mangled self in the wreck of his machine. The voice stopped and the table began to rock back and forth it rose on its own accord, and pinned my friend to the opposite wall. The table dropped down to the floor and we observed that Mrs Campbell was shaking visibly and in a few minutes, she opened her eyes and was back to her normal self. I looked around for my friend but he had fled, presumably back to the safety of the camp.

Dorothy, Mrs Campbell's daughter and myself struck up a warm friendship and the only fly in the ointment was the mother. Although she fully approved of our relationship, when we decided to go out on to the beach, she would bring out her infernal crystal ball remarking that she would be watching our every move. This led to a strained relationship between us and I decided to sever the relationship just in case.

Flying training of the pilots had been intensified and us ground staff put all our efforts into the tasks ahead. The relationship between the pilots and ground crew was excellent, in fact Montrose was a very happy station and morale was high.

That fateful year of 1939 loomed ahead and our Premier Neville Chamberlain had returned from Munich, waving a piece of paper outside Downing Street, 'Peace in our time!'. This however was short lived. Hitler, the corporal painter had moved the Nazi hordes across Europe and had invaded Poland. On 3rd September 1939 a state of war existed between Germany and ourselves. This was the only time that I wept and a flashback of my dream was repeated. The phoney war as we then called it in the initial stages became more evident. There was a considerable amount of activity on the unit. Trenches were being dug, sandbags filled and placed around the slit trenches at strategic points. Carpenters were busy with the manufacture and fitting of detachable frames, covered in a heavy black material for fitment to all the station windows. Air raid drills were carried out, and there was the issue of steel helmets and gas masks.

Our social activities were drastically curtailed, but I had special permission to carry on, as I had joined a civilian dance band as trumpeter. There were four of us, led by a Mrs Scott and I was the only service member of the group. I would be picked up by taxi at 8 pm three times a week and return to base in the early hours of the morning. We would play in the surrounding villages, eightsome reels, including the famous numbers, Dashing White Sergeant, and the Gay Gordons.

One amusing incident occurred which took place at the mental home at Hillside, a few miles from our station. We had finished playing at the home, and I was outside on the balcony, when a male nurse approached in a white coat, and placed his hand on my shoulder. "Time for bed my son." It took a few minutes of fast talking to convince this gentleman that I was a member of the dance band not one of his inmates.

The proceeds of all our engagements were donated to local charities. It proved to be a rewarding pastime.

There is one further incident that I will record. One evening all was quiet in our barrack room, lights were out, the quiet atmosphere was disturbed only by the odd snorer. I had dozed off but suddenly awoke to find standing at the foot of my bed a beautiful apparition of a young girl She was dressed in a white flowing gown and around her slim waist was a golden belt with golden tresses and her head was adorned by a golden crown. She appeared sad and looked into my eyes with compassion and sorrow. She hovered for a few seconds and glided over to the opposite bed. The occupant was an airman, we shall call him AC Rogers. This chap was a loner, with no friends. He was truculent and viewed with suspicion by all the inmates.

The apparition then vanished. I fell into a deep sleep and the next morning I enquired if any of my mates had seen anything odd through the night. Their replies were negative, but I declined to mention my experience of the occult. That day I was extremely quiet and depressed. At 1200 hrs I received a letter in my mail from the relatives of my close buddy Roy Roberts. 'I am sorry to inform you that Roy was killed on a training flight in Canada on take off.'

The second tragedy involved AC Rogers. I had decided to try and make friends with him and I had approached him with the offer of a game of billiards and a meal at the NAAFI that evening, which was on the Friday, but he declined. On the Saturday, Rogers had not been seen. Later that day I enquired at the guardroom as to whether Rogers had booked out but the reply was negative. On the Sunday morning, I noticed that Roger's bed had not been slept in. I immediately reported his absence to the service police. A search party was organised, including a thorough search of the beach. In the sand dunes, neatly stacked was Roger's clothes and pinned to them a note. His body was recovered later, he had committed suicide. My only regret in my ignorance, was that I did not interpret the psychic message and attempt to prevent this tragedy more fully.

The last incident that occurred was as follows: A friend and myself had struck a friendship with two sisters, two Scottish lassies who were employed as maids in a very large mansion on the outskirts of Montrose. The owner, a Scottish army major and his good lady were away and the two sisters invited us to dinner one evening at the mansion. We turned up in uniform and were led to the dining room. Once in our life time we were to be dined with a taste of how the other half lived. The dining table and chairs were antique and on the table was a four place set on a snowy white tablecloth, with the best of silver cutlery. The menu consisted of soup, roast chicken, cheese and biscuits, and coffee. Halfway through the meal a figure appeared at the dining room door and there was the major in full uniform - he had returned unexpectedly. We jumped up to the attention, quaking in our boots. One of the sisters addressed the major: "Sir, our cousins are going overseas and we invited them for a meal. All the food has been paid for." The major disappeared and returned immediately with a bottle of wine. With a wink he smiled and said, "Enjoy yourselves lads." A very understanding chap I thought.

CHAPTER VI

SIGNAL: MOVEMENT TO RAF SPLOTT, CARDIFF

We were in the spring of 1940 and postings were coming in fast. I was to report to RAF Splott, on the outskirts of Cardiff and in the evening there was to be a general get together in the NAAFI. I was loathed to leave Montrose, as I had made many friends.

RAF Splott was approximately a seven mile distance from the city of Cardiff. Cardiff, the capital of Wales was the site of the university and industrial complex on the Bristol channel, which had extensive docks. There was a fine castle of the Norman period or later which is now owned by the City Council. I intended to visit the National Museum of Wales and the St John's Church, which was Perp. with a fine tower. There were fragmentary remains of the Black Friars and Grey Friars Priories.

RAF Splott was isolated and consisted of a large airfield, an administration block and nissen huts to house the service personnel.

On the station was housed Amy Johnson's private plane. Flotating gently were barrage balloons on their lethal steel restraining cables, winch operated, a sure deterrent to any hostile bomber which happened to fly too low.

Around the airfield were manned gunpits, the men drawn from the service personnel on the unit. I was to report to a Sgt Williams in charge of a small detachment. Our function was to modify a few light aircraft, to render them airworthy and to despatch them to various units.

I took an instant dislike to Sgt Williams as he was an autocrat, hell bent on promotion. On his steel helmet he had his name, rank and number stencilled in white and underneath, two crossed spanners. Apart from his odd behaviour, I must admit he was a good and efficient engineer.

Later I was detailed to man one of the gunpits and in position was a Lewis gun. I remember that it was a clear evening. Communications were by means of field telephones, where one would have to furiously turn a handle to magnetise and to transmit our messages to whoever concerned.

In the cloudless sky, with clusters of brilliant blue stars, there was a noise, this was the station siren. There would be the incessant hum of approaching hostile bombers, and there would be the screaming descent of bombs as we received orders on the field telephone to fire.

In the beam of the searchlights, we could see the outline of the bombers, and our guns raked the sky above with tracer bullets. There would be a trail of smoke from the odd bomber, a flash, the rapid nose dive of the bomber, a thud and a sheet of flame, oblivion for the pilot, and a cheer from us gun crews, with the words, "Serve the bastards right!"

There was one incident which could have landed me with a court martial. There was a dance at the officers' mess and I was on guard duty, patrolling the airfield. The time was around 3 am when I heard the sound of an approaching vehicle, its hooded headlights were on dip. I shone my torch, indicating HALT and the vehicle came to a stand still. A man got out from the driver's seat, he was the sole occupant. He was in civilian clothes and as he advanced towards me, I shouted, "Halt, who goes there?. Give the password and advance and be recognised." The figure did not speak but continued to advance and after the third warning I aimed my rifle at his feet and fired. The bullet must have grazed his boot as he stopped in his tracks. It later transpired that he was an army officer and had not heard my instructions, his excuse being that he was slightly deaf. Fortunately he was unmarked but I nevertheless had a good telling off. Although I had obeyed the order to fire after a negative encounter on the third challenge, one cannot go around shooting at officers.

Modifications to the aircraft were proceeding well ahead of schedule and one day I was summoned to the orderly room to receive the good news of my promotion to corporal and the news that I was to relieve Sgt Hunter who was being posted abroad. There were four more aircraft to modify and I was to take charge.

Entertainments at the station were at a low ebb so I decided to rectify this in our favour. I summoned my servicing team and we decided to form an entertainments' committee. We had the go ahead from the station adjutant, our first effort was to have a saturday night dance at the NAAFI canteen. The only snag was that girls were at a premium. Out of the blue I had an inspiration, so I decided to ring up the lady supervisor at the GPO in Cardiff. The reply was promising so we went ahead with our preparations. The great day arrived. One room at the canteen had been transformed. With coloured streamers and balloons hanging from the ceiling, the portable bar, which had been set up and the makeshift stage at one end all was ready. First to arrive was a six piece band followed by the married airmen with their wives. The time was now around 9 pm and the single airmen including myself were drinking at the bar. My party had not turned up and we thought that the dance would be a washout as far as we were concerned. A few minutes later, the entertainments' officer arrived with a smile, "Lewis', he said, "At the double to the guardroom, there is a surprise package at the gates." I was greeted by a lady who informed me that she was the supervisor of the telephone exchange in Cardiff and that the girls were waiting. There were twenty five ladies in the coach and I wasted no time in escorting them to the canteen. I remember well the look of amazement as they entered and the band stopped playing. There was a great cheer from the single lads, but not a word from the married families. I thought to myself, "That will cut the ground from under you my beauties," as I glanced at the wives. If any of these warm hearted ladies of the exchange, particularly the supervisor happen to read this book, we wish to thank them for their warm hearted gesture, in relieving the boredom of the airmens' lot.

One other pleasurable social event which we attended at Cardiff, was the Sunday visit to the chapel named 'Tabernacle', under the able guidance of the reverend minister Myrddin Davies, in community hymn singing, directed at Hitler and company.

The day arrived when the last of the four aircraft had been modified and my last task there prior to posting was to complete all the paperwork and log books and despatch the aircraft as directed. We were now in the spring of 1942 and our postings came through. I was to be posted to Talbenny, near Milford Haven.

CHAPTER VII

FERRY TRAINING UNIT, RAF TALBENNY, No 303

Situated 4 miles NW of Milford Haven, a bleak airfield overlooking St. Bridges Bay, having three runways with a central intersection, two T2 hangars and 36 frying pan hard standings. Later in the war it became a transport command base and additional aprons were added to accommodate 22 aircraft.

In May 1942 it became a coastal command station in 19 Group. The Wellingtons of 311 Czech Squadron arrived on the 12 June 304 Polish Squadron arrived simultaneously. I understand that the Czech Minister of National Defence Mr. Masaryk, the Foreign Minister and the Czech Deputy Prime Minister visited 311 Czech Squadron to mark its second anniversary.

It was in 1943/44 that the squadron left Talbenny and was replaced by 303 Ferry Training Unit, which flew its Wellingtons down from Stornoway. This unit's task was to prepare aircraft for overseas, these included Wellingtons, Warwicks, and Venturas. It was here that we were introduced to a new dimension, the arrival of WAAFS, posted in to take over all kinds of posts. My duties here would be to service and despatch aircraft. Milford Haven boasted a naval base and a trawler fishing port, with one of the largest natural harbours in Britain. Deposited in the modern church was a Bible and Prayer Book donated by Lord Nelson. There was also a large all services' club at Milford Haven and it was here that I learned to play chess from the experts.

It was also at RAF Talbenny, that I had my first encounter with the WAAFS that fine body of womanhood doing a man's job. They carried out their tasks as administrators, technicians and transport drivers. I took special note of the airmens' appearance - they were smartly groomed and their language controlled when in contact with the fair sex. I had to get used to the practice of saluting the WAAF officers and calling them 'MAAM'. There were several national service airmen and reservists drawn from civilian life such as bankers, clerks, company directors and so forth and there would be the odd one, who would resent the imposed discipline experienced in service life. Most of the ferrying pilots were in their teens, competent and a mutual respect between them and the ground staff was apparent to all.

Pilots would distribute to the ground staff their unused clothing coupons, duty free tobacco, and nylons to be used as gifts for our relatives and girl friends. I received seven days leave and proceeded to Ffestiniog, to find that two of my brothers had volunteered for the RAF. Jack had enlisted as an armourer and Leslie in the equipment branch.

27

There were new faces around the village, these were the evacuees and the villagers were doing their utmost to settle them into the community.

On my arrival at base, on completion of leave, I was informed that my posting had come through. This was to prove to be exciting and dangerous, and would be of 2-3 years duration.

My posting was to RAF Honington of No 3 Group Bomber Command, under the expert leadership of that famous AVM Bomber Harris.

CHAPTER VIII

RAF HONINGTON 3 GROUP BOMBER COMMAND

RAF Honington is approximately 3 miles from the town of Thetford, in East Anglia, and is worthy of a visit. Thetford lay on the edge of Breckland. There were remains of a priory and an abbey (AM). The huge conical castle mound was approximately 81 feet high. Of 20 former old churches only three now remain, Norm. and Perp. and under the tall tower lies the Norman font. The King's House was once the hunting lodge of King James I and the tudor 'Bell Inn' was very picturesque. The 15th century ancient house is now a museum. There was also an ancient lock up with the stocks. Thomas Paine, author of 'The Rights of Man' was born here in 1737. The newly afforested Thetford Chase lies to the west.

I was posted to No 9 squadron based at Honington which came under No 3 Group Bomber Command. The Dunkurk catastrophy in 1940 saw the remnants of Nos 103 and 105 squadrons arriving at Honington and reforming there in July 1940. New faces arrived on the scene, those of Czech airmen from France to fight with the allies. They were formed into 311 Czech squadron, utilising both their base at Honington and the satellite at East Wretham in September 1940. Aircraft used were the Wellingtons, MK ICs and IIs and later the MK IIIs. No 9 squadron was the first to be equipped with the MK IIIs which were powered with Hercules engines.

Honington was a well established pre-war RAF base. A neat and well planned complex. Living quarters were in red bricked, heated blocks. It had a large square, used for ceremonial parades which was dominated on the one end with the RAF flag and the other end with the Administration Block. The airmens' mess was also near the quarters and the air raid shelters. The airfield was very large and leading from it were tarmacadam paths to accommodate the transportation of the bomber aircraft to their dispersal points on hard standings, admirably camouflaged with their brown and green striped upper surfaces and sides in dope paint. They would be undetectable on their hard standings on the edge of the forest nearby from the air. The aircraft were the Wellington bombers affectionately dubbed the 'Flying Pigs' by the ground crew.

I was to be attached to 311 Czech squadron, manned by British and those gallant freedom fighters the Czech air crews. The 311 Squadron Czech commanding officer was Sqn Ldr Brietzetel who was instrumental in recommending my promotion to sergeant but more of this later.

The integration of the British and Czech ground crews resulted in mutual respect and comradeship. Language difficulties were resolved by learning the basic essentials in English or Czech, essential to servicing the bombers and so forth. Briefly the construction of the airframes were geodetic and powered by merlin engines, mounted on the port and starboard wings. The undercarriages were hydraulically operated from the cockpit. The ailerons on the wings housed flaps which were recessed on their trailing edges and were variable and controlled hydraulically from the pilot's cockpit. These were adjusted in the air to correct lateral trim and also the same principals were used to correct longitudinal trim by the fitment of elevator flaps or tabs at the rear of the elevators. The tail wheel was also operated from the cockpit and when in the air, the landing gear would be retracted to give a streamline profile to the relative airflow. The bomb doors under the belly of the aircraft were also hydraulically operated and they housed the 250 and 500lb bombs. The most isolated of the crew, was the airgunner. These brave lads would be very confined in their turrets.

I was to be the corporal in charge of three Wellingtons, which included 'F' for Freddie, the Czech commanding officer, Sqn Ldr Brietzetel's bomber and I ensured that the aircraft I had been allocated were always in a state of readiness and airworthiness. Our own free time was of no importance and the ground crew and myself would spend long hours into dawn at the disperal points to ensure that all was in order for the take off and return from missions over Germany.

One amusing scenario resulted from our scrounging bacon ribs from the cook in the airmen's mess. Having converted a five gallon drum to act as a stove at the dispersal points we would fuel it with wood and place a couple of metal rods across the open tops. Suspended from these by a thin wire, would be the bacon ribs, they would be barbecued and the aroma and taste would be the envy of any modern chef. Portions of the ribs were allocated to the aircrew and it was amusing to watch the pilots taxying their aircraft nibbling away at their ribs.

Esprit-de-corps and morale was extremely high at this station and only one personal unpleasant incident occurred here. The British Warrant Officer in charge of the squadron had become extremely hostile towards me, the reasons were as follows.

One day he called me into his office and came straight to the point. "Cpl Lewis, if you think that you are to be recommended to sergeant over the head of Corporal Saunders (ex Halton brat), you can think again." The atmosphere in his office was thick and after a few heated words, he said, "Step outside and fight." If I had taken advantage of his aggressive attitude I would have been court martialled for striking a superior officer. He was a clever chap as all our conversation was in the privacy of his office. I immediately turned on my heel, fuming, and my parting shot was, "Get stuffed warrant officer!" A few days later I was called in to the station adjutant's office to be informed that I had been promoted to sergeant and that the warrant officer had been posted. I was to meet up with this character again after the war, in Germany.

One afternoon four of us were making our way from the dispersal points to the airmens' mess for tea. That morning over the radio we had heard the voice of William Joyce, that British traitor on 'Germany calling, Germany calling'. In his effeminate voice, one sentence stood out. "We know that you are visiting Honington Dr Benes (the Czechoslovakian President) and we will give you a warm reception." As we proceeded to the airmens' mess, I happened to glance towards one of the airmens' blocks. The air had gone extremely cold and my three comrades were shivering. In the gathering gloom, I saw an apparition gliding and encircling the block. I said to my mates, "Look over there, what can you see?" They remarked, "Nothing, sarge." I fell silent.

We were a few yards from the mess when we heard the drone of three aircraft and directly overhead and very low, were these aircraft which we thought were Blenheims. I noticed that the bomb doors were open and could just make out the markings. I said to my mates, "These are bloody jerries," we broke into a gallop and slid down into the nearest air raid shelter. There was no warning of hostile aircraft approaching and the series of coloured flags to indicate yellow for warning, red for overhead and white for all clear were conspicuous by their absence. This was to be our first experience of war but would be followed by many more.

As we crouched in the shelter we heard the distinct rattle of machine gun fire, followed by the peculiar sound of a high pitched whine as the bombs were released. The air raid shelter would visibly shake, the feeling was as if thousands of tons of water were being dropped on our shelter.

It was then in the moment of truth that we prayed that we would not sustain a direct hit. As suddenly as it had begun, all was quiet. I cautiously opened the heavy steel door of the shelter and proceeded up the steps. The damage caused to buildings was severe. The barrack block where I had seen the apparition had been devastated but surprisingly the number of casualties were low. We ran to the dispersals to see if our bombers had been damaged but all was normal. It appeared that the enemy pilots were concentrating on the admin area and possibly Dr Benes but he had already left the station.

The only other damage sustained was a few bomb craters on the airfield. It appeared that our station had become a prime target and due to the presence of the Czech squadron which must have incensed our fat friend Marshal Herman Goering of the Luftwaffe the bombing raids became more frequent.

There were times when the enemy bombers would be overhead before we had adequate warning of their presence and on subsequent raids we began to associate the very high pitched screeching of the pheasants in the surrounding forests with a raid. This would occur perhaps one hour before the bombers were overhead and we would identify this phenomenon with a hostile visit and would prepare accordingly. I am sure that these beloved birds saved many a casualty and to this day I treat them with the respect and affection they deserve. On the daylight raids most of the servicing teams would stay in the shelters at the dispersal points to be ready for the immediate take off of the aircraft and to be on instant standby.

I remember on one occasion, a raid was in progress at daybreak. It was a misty morning. Four enemy bombers approached, the target was RAF Honington again and they made their run over the forest, the camouflaged aircraft and our shelters.

From a safe vantage point within the confines of the shelter, I volunteered to keep a cautious look out as an observer, unofficial of course, and I witnessed the bombs coming down. I was surprised to note that they did not go off on the first impact with the ground, but would bounce along and go off on the third or fourth bounce. My attention was suddenly diverted to two young airmen running towards our shelter. Suddenly they both fell down the shelter steps. I caught one of them and brought him into the shelter but he was dead with shrapnel wounds to his stomach. His brother died later in hospital with gunshot wounds. I learned later that the two brothers were twins and that they had only recently been posted to the station.

The raids had become so frequent and the casualties were rising all the time that slit trenches were hastily dug outside the station perimeter and apart from a few of us who had to remain at the dispersal points with our aircraft non essential personnel would make for the slit trenches.

There was a friendly rivalry between the ground crews and the SNCO's of each 'Flight' for the distinction of having all their aircraft fully serviceable and operational for immediate take off. Each of the ground crews of their respective flights would re-double their efforts to ensure that the aircraft which had returned from their mission over Germany were quickly and efficiently repaired from flak and shrapnel damage which would involve around the clock repairs to be ready for the next planned operation.

One of the awards was that the SNCO IC flight, who failed to render a 100% serviceability for the next mission would have to dig deep into his pocket to fork out cash to pay for a round of drinks for all the ground staff squadron so standards were high, quick and efficient.

One day our squadron was to fly on a mission, over Bremen and the aircraft were to be ready for take off by 2200hrs that evening. At 2100hrs one of my corporals reported that one the Wimpey's, 'C' for Charlie was unserviceable. The hydraulic system that operated the trimming tabs had air in the system which would require bleeding. I grabbed my tool box and we set to work. We were nearly finished when the Czech flight crew arrived. The only remaining task was for me to enter the aircraft and lock up the bleeder screws on the master cylinder with soft mild steel wire. By this time the aircraft was taxying to the take off position and as I lay crouched in the centre of the aircraft fuselage there was a sudden increase in revs, a sudden surge forward. I realised my predicament and would have been airborne except that one of the crew noticed the presence of a reluctant addition to the crew so take off was aborted. There was one major defect on the Wimpeys. Particularly on the earlier types, the MK I and MK II. The wings would drop off in flight so there was intense activity to determine the cause. I was chosen to proceed to AHQ in the south of England to represent our station. The cause of the wing failure was a series of hairline cracks, located at the root end housing which located the ratchet bolts. These were checked by magnifying glass on all the Wimpeys at base. The maximum number of cracks and the length and depth of the cracks considered safe had been pre determined and all wings housing hairline cracks in excess of this number, would be scrapped.

CHAPTER IX

RAF EAST WRETHAM - SATELLITE OF RAF HONINGTON

Cliff soon discovered how primitive were the living conditions on the airfield. On its outskirts were a series of tents hastily erected to house the military personnel of the army and airmen to be deployed on the airfield. Officers and a very few SNCO's were housed in a few scattered permanent buildings which included the odd nissen hut etc. Just as we arrived a Dornier 17 came out of the clouds and circled. The air defences opened up and promptly the Dornier pilot had second thoughts, consequently he turned sharply to starboard and headed in the direction of Honington, where he dropped eight delayed action bombs on the airfield. This was the pilots error of judgement as he could not have chosen a worse target, the ground-to-air defences latched on to his aircraft immediately and brought it down at Bury St Edmunds. The task of teaching the Czech pilots to convert to Wellingtons was left in the capable hands of Flt Lt P C Pickard who was destined for higher acclaim, we the ground crew were priviliged to serve under his leadership.

The first operational sorties were made on 10th Sept 1940 with Brussels as the main target. A few days later, the now fully trained Czech pilots and other air crews took part in many raids from Wretham and their base at Honington.

One incident involved three Wellingtons which were being despatched to Mannheim. As the third aircraft took off it circled low to land again but instead crashed in flames on the outskirts of Wretham and the Wretham Hall road, detonating its bomb load. I was in charge of the recovery party. During the winter months of 1940/41 enemy raiders were continuously in the Wretham area, by day and night. Twenty bombs were dropped on the 3rd Feb 1941 of which 13 landed on the airfield, resulting in one damaged Wellington. On the 3rd March during night flying, one Wellington of 311 Squadron that was airborne was followed by a Junker 88 and 10 bombs were dropped in the process and on the 8th April another Junker 88 shot down a Wellington again on night flying over the airfield. No 311 Czech Squadron operated from East Wretham against a number of targets and in May the squadron was transferred to RAF Aldergrove.

The village of East Wretham boasted a Post Office which was run by a well known beloved and respected family by the name of Brown. The only public house was very old and full of character and to this day there can still be seen World War II framed pictures of this friendly Inn.

The locals were a shy retiring community with a good sense of

34

humour and we slotted in nicely with these wonderful people.

As previously mentioned, the living conditions on the airfield were primitive with the exception of a few wooden buildings and the odd nissen huts with their usual coke burning cylindrical iron stoves with their stack pipe chimneys belching out smoke in the initial stages of burning. The old basic cast iron beds were prominently displayed, complete with their straw filled palliases, compacted with the passage of time. The administrative building was a makeshift affair located to the edge of the airfield. The Wimpeys were neatly parked on their own hard standing pans, camouflaged in dark brown and green, blending with the earth and green of the encircling forest. The walls of some of the buildings had been transformed with colourful painted murals by the artistic members of the Czech airmen and depicted scenes form Czechoslovakia, this was a boost to morale. Some of the Czech crews never came back from their operational sorties.

One fatal tragedy had a traumatic effect on the servicing ground crew. A young British airman, in the trade of armourer, had just landed from a practice flight, and had only recently been posted in, when he climbed down the metal ladder under the nose of the Wimpey and instead of proceeding to the rear of the aircraft, turned and walked directly into the path of the starboard propeller mounted on the wing, which was being shut down. The airman swayed for a few seconds, then landed at my feet. I shall not go into details, but I picked him up gently and laid him down, covering him with my brown dust coat. I ran to inform the flight commander, who immediately phoned for the doctor and an ambulance. He was later transferred to the station morgue, and I in turn was violently sick.

A few days later, I was detailed as SNCO I/C recovery crash party, involving a crashed Wellington. The devastation within the area of the crash was a nightmare. We were working in the glow of lamps which threw a golden light over the wreckage. There was a large pool of slimy green water. Our first duty was to retrieve the flight crew remains and we worked feverishly through the long night, again, I shall not go into details of the conditions prevailing. Another incident that occurred involved one of the corporals who was of a nervous disposition. He returned from leave and was one of the fortunate who had accommodation in one of the nissen huts. He arrived when it was dark and rather than show a light and disturb his comrades, he cautiously made his way to his bed space, which was immediately behind the entrance door. Being very tired he dropped off to sleep, awaking in the early hours of the morning but instead of greetings from his comrades, he was confronted with a line up of six coffins, draped with Union Jacks up the aisle of the barrack room. The corporal hurriedly dressed and reported the incident to me and was shaken in the process.

One of the most dangerous tasks that confronted the ground crews, was the extinguishing of the flare path oil lamps. When the bombers returned from their nightly missions over Germany, they would be followed by hostile enemy aircraft. Using the flare path as a ground marker, they would rake the airfield with gunfire, anti-personnel bombs and other high explosive devices. It was on such an occasion one evening that I was the SNCO on duty. Towards the early hours of the morning there was the incessant hum of our returning bombers. The pheasants in the woods were quiet. It was my turn to put out the flares. As directed by flying control the signal given would be a red light and when the last bomber was overhead, I proceeded onto the airfield, armed with a spade to dig myself in, a steel helmet and a bicylce. There were three of us ground crew on the same task. The last bomber had just arrived and had landed. The red light flashed from flying control so we commenced dousing the lights. Whilst on the centre of this lonely and vast airfield, we heard a sudden chattering of the pheasants, and within minutes, the familiar drone of enemy aircraft. We had another twelve lamps to extinguish but the enemy was immediately overhead. It was too late to either run or dig ourselves in and the airfield became alive with the thud of bombs and gunfire.

We laid flat on the airfield daring not to move a muscle when suddenly there was a dead calm.. We hurriedly extinguished the remaining oil lamps and reported to flying control. Except for damage to one aircraft and a few localised fires, damage was comparatively light under the circumstances. Of the aircraft that returned two had made a forced landing on our southern coast and three had failed to return. The most pathetic and touching scenes at this unit, were the looks of despair on the faces of the wives who were at the airfield to greet their husbands on their return from a mission only to be told that the aircraft would not be returning and that the collection of the aircrews' belongings would be from the officers' and sergeants' messes.

There is one other incident which I must record. One of our corporals, a keen gardener, was busily digging the small border outside his bunk when he came across a skeleton, buried in a shallow grave. The police were called and it transpired that the remains were that of a woman who had been reported missing twenty years previously. There was a large hole in the skull made by a blunt instrument. We did not hear any follow up details on this particular find.

The great day arrived when a signal was received to prepare all available bombers for the 1,000 bomber raid. The station was a beehive of activity with the continuous flow of tractors and low trailers, delivering 500lb bombs for loading into the bellies of the Wellingtons.

At last the signal came for operational standby and then they were away. They took off in a continual stream and we that were left watched with humility and perhaps a touch of sadness on what must be done. On that memorable day, our squadron suffered casualties and a few days later, I was informed that I was to be posted overseas and was granted leave.

Prior to this, I was summoned into the station commander's office and informed that I had been mentioned in Despatches and that there had been an article published in the 'London Gazette'. Although I had rescued together with other ground crew, the occupants of a burning plane and a four year old boy from a water hydrant, which was all in the line of duty anyway, I was presented with the oak leaf. I had not expected any reward considering what the aircrew were subjected to.

Having said farewell to all my colleagues, and those gallant aircrews, I picked up my travelling documents and was homeward bound. There was little change in our little village of Ffestiniog, but perhaps it was more austere with ration books and clothing coupons, but I was pleased to note that the refugees from the great cities were settling into the community and many of them did in fact remained there after the war. One of the great events, centred around the chapels, particularly in Blaenau Ffestiniog, was the community hymn singing. Large crowds would congregate inside and outside the chapels to participate and to listen. Visitors passing through would stop and the English residents would marvel at the depth of feeling portrayed on these occasions. One day whilst on a weekend trip to Blackpool, I decided to give Gypsy Rose Lee a vist. I was in civilian clothes and entered the consulting room of this famous lady.

She predicted that I was a member of the Armed Forces and would be on a journey travelling by sea and air to Egypt and England. On my return I would marry a foreign girl and have two sons who would be of an academic nature. This was later proved to be true. I married a Finnish girl had two sons, the eldest, John, and the youngest, Michael, both who obtained degrees at Bristol University. John became a Phd. - Doctor of Philosophy and the youngest, Michael, obtained a Batchelor of Science honours degree.

All this of course would be in the future many years hence. On my return to Ffestiniog from my mini weekend in Blackpool, there was the usual buff coloured envelope, OHMS, awaiting my attention. My posting instructions had come through and it was to a holding unit in Egypt, pending posting elsewhere. We were to assemble in Liverpool and then make our way to the Hook of Holland. The troop train was full of the three services personnel and on arrival at the Hook of Holland, we disembarked. We were directed to field kitchens where we had a meal, a wash and brush up and then on to the the makeshift cinema and the sergeants' mess.

My recollections of the events following our visit to the mess are as follows. We decided to sample all the spirits on display at sixpence a tot and later we were in a highly intoxicated state. I did not make the cinema.

Two companions and myself apparently had been picked out of the gutter and carried to the troop train and unceremoniously bundled on to the roof racks in the train compartments. This particular troop train was the Medlock 'C' route train to Trieste. There were two engines attached for the heavy drag up the alps. Days later, and much bemused, I arrived at Trieste. We formed units and marched to the airfield where we were uplifted to the various destinations.

CHAPTER X

RAF STAGING POST, LUQA, GEORGE CROSS ISLAND OF MALTA

The holding unit was a small outpost within the Canal Zone and all the buildings were semi-permanent, made of canvas. There was one large tent, which served as a mess and bar. There were waiters in galobiers, a white gown type of dress which flowed to their ankles. They wore sandals, and their head gear was a red fez. They looked cool in the excessive, humid heat of the desert. We had been kitted out with KD, thin khaki drill uniforms which were comfortable, and easy to wear. Drinks were served in green glasses, which had been cut in half from bottles, by the enterprising waiters. The beer was ice cool and that famous toxic brew, peculiar to Egypt, brewed in Cairo, by the name of Stella Artois, was strong. The after effect was a splitting headache.

Postings were coming in thick and fast when mine eventually came through. I was to be posted to RAF Luqua in Malta which was nearer to England. This was to be the 'George Cross Island' and I was to proceed by air. That evening we had a large party at the mess, with the remainder of the personnel, awaiting postings. To the east of the holding unit, was the RAF station of El-Firdan, a unit I would be posted to in later years and where I was to witness terrorism at its worst and my own brush with death from near drowning.

We arrived at Malta in the heat of a summer's day and landed at Luqa airport. I was to be attached to 64 SP (Staging Post), and my function there would be to take charge and service both military and civilian Dakotas the DC4s and to change the ration boxes of service personnel in transit.

The Maltese Islands are in a strategic position in the central Mediterannean with excellent natural harbours and have been occupied by successive powers from the Phoenicians to the British. There was the great siege in the sixteenth century when the knights of St.John ruled and their heroic strength in the present struggle in the Second World War and their progression towards independence which was to come later in 1964.

The capital city of Malta was Valletta, with its tier of neat white houses and the magnificent buildings above massive ramparts, flanked by the 'Grand Harbour' and the deep water creeks dividing the ancient cities of Vittoriosa and Senglea. Nearby was also the town of Sliema and the blue bays of St.George and St.Julian.

The Maltese people are somewhat short in stature, stocky, swarthy and sturdy in gait. Their language is Semetic, originally a Punic dialect, no doubt influenced by the Arabs. They also have a good command of the English language. The Maltese Islands are the most populated in the Mediterranean.

The continental masses nearest to the Maltese Islands are Scicily, approximately 58 miles and Tunisia, 180 miles. To the east is the Suez Canal and to the west, the straits of Gibraltar, each 1,000 miles distant. Across the shimmering haze of the blue water, is the island of Gozo.

Recessed on the outside walls of many of the houses were apertures which housed beautiful religious relics in particular The Virgin Mary, painted in vivid colours. Here, one can see the many religious processions and 'Fiestas'.

There were many German and Italian prisoners of war housed and surrounded by barbed wire fences. Rumour had it from one of the senior German officers that they were going to rebuild the island and restore it to its former glory.

Here too was the famous 'Gut', a narrow street, with shops and cobbled, stepped roads. Here one would find certain members of the fair sex, plying their trade in the world's oldest profession.

Our living quarters were in wooden huts away from the main RAF base at Luqa and we had our own mess in yet another wooden building.

Nearby was the pathetic 'Leper Colony' where one could observe at close quarters the ravages of the dreaded disease. In Sliema there would be the dreaded black cross painted on the outside of isolated houses and the thick lime covered paths leading to these houses. This was the sign of the isolation of the unfortunate occupants, who had caught the equally dreaded disease, the Bubonic Plague.

My Technical Officer was Flying officer French, he was young and of fresh complexion. He had recently graduated but had very limited practical experience of aircraft servicing. To give the gentleman his due however, he was as hot as mustard on the 'Administrative' side, much to the discomfort of the airmen in general. On the disciplinary side, he would pull up airmen for long hair, dirty boots and greasy overalls, particularly when they were involved in the intricate servicing of the aircraft. He had many F252 the old familiar charge forms to his dubious credit.

One day I was called into his office and he pointed to a dagger which had impaled a square of paper with his name on it and was embedded on his office desk. "Sergeant Lewis, do you think it is meant for me?" I quickly assured him that it was a practical joke laid on by an inebriated airman. He dismissed me and wiping his brow, said, "I do not wish to be disturbed for the next hour." Perhaps he was going through the long list of charges, past and present to narrow down the name of his suspect. My prime suspect was AC Davidson, a morose and sullen airman and disliked by many of the ground crew staff.

One evening whilst we were on night shift, the ground crew of my shift were sitting on their tool boxes, awaiting the next batch of aircraft. The aircraft duly arrived and I ordered my crew to get cracking and service them. AC Davidson refused to budge off his tool box and after the third refusal, I decided to call in the orderly officer, who happened to be Fg Off French. He arrived at the double, I'm sure he must have sprinted from the mess as he arrived mopping his brow. I explained to him that Davidson had refused to service aircraft. At the back of my mind was the paragraph dealing with 'Mutiny' in King's rules and Air Council Instructions (KRs and ACIs).

The officer decided to try his luck and after the third refusal, instructed me to place him under 'Close Arrest.'

As he marched under escort to the guardroom he muttered audibly "If you lot think I am going to service aircraft carrying civilian passengers," (he had the mistaken idea, that senior officers were shareholders), "you have another think coming." His parting shot referred to the dagger. Only the officer and I knew of it at the time so here was the suspect.

In the next couple of days I saw the fastest posting in my service career. There was Davidson, complete with his kit, earmarked for a spell of duty at RAF Sharga, in the Gulf a very hot and sticky climate where he would have time to reflect on his stupid behaviour and it was of the general opinion that he was fortunate not to have been court martialled.

We are now in the final phase of the war in Europe and three of us SNCOs were recommended to attend a commissioning board, from 216 AHQ Egypt which convened at our base of Luqa. Two of us passed the board, a Flight Sergeant Ralph and myself and instructions were to follow, for OCTU (Officer Conversion Training Unit) in the UK. In the interim period a signal was received that there would be several VIPs arriving. The base was a beehive of activity until the day dawned for their reception.

First to arrive by warship was the first of our distinguished visitors no other than the President of the United States, F D Roosevelt who was quickly followed by our beloved 'Premier', Winston Churchill, by air. His aircraft was parked outside flying control and waiting directly in front of the aircraft was the Guard of Honour, in the presence of the Governor of the Island. We shall come back to this later. The next Liberator to arrive was the one conveying that immaculate gentleman the Foreign Secretary, Anthony Eden.

I was present when he disembarked but unfortunately he slipped and I jumped forward to break his fall. He thanked me for the prompt action taken and he remarked that he could have broken an ankle.

Having arranged the ground crew to service the aircraft, I hurried to flying control but there was still no sign of the Premier alighting from the aircraft. The Guard of Honour were perspiring profusely and were becoming restive. Suddenly the door opened and a steward in white jacket appeared and said, "Come back later, the Prime Minister is asleep."

I do not think that this little episode went down very well with the Governor or the Guard of Honour.

The VIPs were here as the prelude to the Yalta Conference and they were to fly in an aircraft heavily guarded by a ring of steel helmeted American and British soldiers.

We are now well into 1945 and there was a certain and definable air of a momentous announcement to be made.

A signal had been received that Flight Sergeant Ralph and myself were to proceed immediately to the UK and were to embark the following day on a troopship to report to OCTU for officer training in the UK.

The great day arrived and we were safely on the troopship when another signal was received. It was VE day with the cessation of hostilities in Europe and we were to disembark immediately. We were extremely disappointed to learn later that our OCTU had been cancelled but overjoyed to hear that the war in Europe had come to an end.

The Island went mad with rejoicing - flags, bunting, beer and wine were flowing freely in the messes and Fred Grace the lightweight champion boxer who had retired from boxing and was employed on the Island with a British steel company, maintaining the feeder pipes from shore to convey oil to ships at various terminals was rejoicing with the rest of us. I had befriended him and he was busy at the sergeants' mess piano. He was an accomplished pianist turning out scores of Sousas military marches to an enthusiastic audience.

A general directive from Command was posted on various notice boards at base which could have a profound effect on our service career. The gist was this: Due to the contraction within the aircraft engineering branch, we were urged to consider remustering to the 'Mechanical Transport Trade' but still to remain Group I and were advised that promotion prospects would be better.

After a lot of heart searching and consultations with fellow SNCOs a few of us decided to apply for transport, and having been accepted we would be posted to Royal Air Force Weeton, for an intensive course on mechanical transport engineering.

We said goodbye to the beautiful island of Malta and the many friends that we had made there.

Entrance to Valetta. Malta, 1945

St Peters and St Paul 'Rabat'. Malta, 1945

Southern view of Valetta. Malta, 1945

Section of Servicing Crew, 64SP. Malta, 1945

Group photograph of Flight Riggers and Mech,E's of 64SP. Halfar, Malta, 1945

CHAPTER XI

S of TT (SCHOOL OF TECHNICAL TRAINING), RAF WEETON

RAF Weeton was a highly organised MT training station, complete with qualified staff of service and civilian instructors and was also the trade standards base for both drivers and MT engineers. Here one could also qualify for MOT examiners and driving instructors.

We were to report to the training officer of S of TT (School of Technical Training). The station was comfortable and we were billeted in modern central heated blocks and each SNCO had his own spacious bunk. Parades were minimal but I was determined to join the station military band and learn to play another instrument having previously mastered the trumpet - the instrument I chose was the Tenor Horn in 'E flat'.

Weeton was based within a few miles of Kirkham village and a few miles from my favourite seaside resort of Blackpool, which had excellent sands, bathing and fishing. Amusements here are on a vast scale. Blackpool embraces the golden mile. The well known tower rises to over 500ft. A mere 3.5 miles away is Poulton-Le-Fylde and one of the interesting features here are the stocks and whipping post in the old market place. There is also a stepped Jacobean pillar and ancient fish-stones where prices were once fixed. In the church are two richly carved chairs and a fine carved screen.

Within a short motoring distance is the resort of Lytham-St-Annes and a few miles further afield, Southport, Preston and Wigan. Yes, we were ideally and strategically placed with all the social amenities at our fingertips. The course was going well, which embraced all aspects of mechanical transport engineering and the course was divided into basic, chassis, steering, transmissions, gear boxes and electrical systems.

One of the most impressive ceremonies was the annual church parade and remembrance at Blackpool. As a member of the station band, the moving ceremony at the cenotaph with the band marching to the military score of the 'Standard of St.George' and 'Imperial Echoes', brought back memories of fallen comrades. On the social side, dances were held in the sergeants' mess and we were amply rewarded by the attendance of some of the 'Blackpool Landladies' and they were great fun to be with.

One of the most degrading aspects of service life, was to witness warrant officers and SNCOS' of the air crew, those gallant and brave individuals, having to revert by day to their basic trade and work in overalls, covering their badges of rank but reverting to their aircrew rank after working hours. I do not know which member of the 'Air Council' thought this feather brained scheme up. In my opinion it lowered morale, far better to demob this gallant body of men.

The course was going well and we were in the final stages when the day dawned for our finals. I passed with a satisfying mark of 85%.
A directive had been issued from Command, introducing technician ranks this would mean that the badges of rank of NCOs would be inverted whilst those that elected for the command side would wear their badges of rank the right way up. I decided to opt for the command side. I was not to know at this early stage that promotion in the MT trade was to be a long and delayed struggle. My posting eventually came through, and this was to an RAF station, by the name of Royal Air Force Llanbedr, a mere 14 miles distance from my home village of Ffestiniog.

Servicing Personnel, 64 SP. RAF Halfar, Malta. Top Row: 5th from Left Cpl Glover, outstanding NCO. 1945

Servicing Personnel relaxing. Swimming in harbour. Malta, 1945

Royal Naval vessels at anchor in Malta Grand Harbour, 1945

HRH Princess Margaret 'Countess of Snowdon', relaxing after presenting the Standards to No.80 & 218 Sqdn's at RAF Bruggen. 15th July, 1964

Section of Dance Band. RAF El-Firdan, Egypt.
Cpl Washer, founder, standing playing the
Double Bass. 1952

Servicing Crew. Cpl Hogg in charge, 6th
from the Left. Aircraft - DC4, 64SP RAF
Halfar. Malta, 1945

CHAPTER XII

RAF LLANBEDR, GWYNEDD, NORTH WALES

One of the finest locations in Britain, Llanbedr is shown as a narrow coastal strip, nestling between the mountains, just to the east of Harlech Castle. The airfield was opened in June 1941 and was initially under the control of RAF Valley, as a forward airfield for day operations against enemy aircraft in the Irish sea. A succession of squadrons were posted in to Llanbedr, some for very short duration. No 631 Squadron of Spitfires was resident when I was posted in to take charge of the MT servicing in 1948 and in 1949. 631 Squadron was re-numbered 20 Squadron and was eventually disbanded in 1951.

Llanbedr itself was a small isolated village consisting of a few houses with the RAF station on its outskirts. This was a split affair. On one side were a few wooden huts serving as living accommodation and on the other side, was a small airfield with the MT section and station workshops nearby.

The pace here was slow and leisurely and a few miles distant was Harlech with its 13th century castle and notable gateway, situated on Tremadoc Bay with a wide view of the Snowdonia Mountains. From here one can cross over the toll bridge to the town of 'Portmadoc' a small seaport and industrial town with its sandy beaches amongst rocks. The flat expanse of Traeth Mawr is backed by the Moelwyns, Cynicht and the Snowdon Range. The newly re-opened Ffestiniog railway extends from here into the Vale of Ffestiniog.

Nearby is Maentwrog in the Vale of Ffestiniog with views of the twin Moelwyns, and the sharp peak of Cynicht. About two miles south are the Rhaiadr Ddu and Raven Waterfalls.

Working conditions here were excellent, in as much that we had the MT section split into two parts. The driving side had in charge my opposite number, a flight sergeant, who we shall call Lee. I was to take charge of the MT servicing and had a capable corporal by the name of Cpl Lewis and a staff of eight airmen. Due to the lack of accommodation at the unit, I was permitted to commute daily from my home, with the proviso that I had reliable transport. I obtained it as follows: I overheard in conversation, that a local farmer had an old 1933 Morris Minor for sale and I decided to visit him, together with Cpl Lewis.

We arrived at the farm and were directed to a barn. Inside was the Morris Minor and the sole occupants in the vehicle were a brood of hens. Having chased them out, we got down to business. Whilst the farmer was starting it up, my corporal was busy at the rear, tapping the wing and shouting to the farmer. "We have a knock here," indicating that the engine was not functioning as it should and, "the big ends are going." With this somewhat devious approach, we obtained the car for twenty five pounds. It was already taxed and insured and we drove it away but a few yards from the camp the battery fell out which was under the driver's seat so in effect a knock did develop. We hurried back to the farmer to obtain our money back but with a twinkle in his eye, the farmer said, "I knew that your colleague was knocking the wing at the rear and a bargain is a bargain." We then had the damned car towed to a garage to put it right.

As MT controller, I was in a good position. The squadron leader, let us call him, Squadron Leader Thomas, a gentleman of the old school and nearing retirement, was in charge of the MT section. One day he asked if I could move a half circular nissen hut, complete to the other side of the runway. I said it could be done.

The following morning a gang of us hoisted the nissen hut by Coles crane on to two bogeys, ie four wheeled short trailers, fore and aft and together with a tractor, we proceeded slowly along the runway to its new location. The previous evening there was an officers' mess party and at breakfast next morning a young juniorg officer was gazing out of the dining room window overlooking the runway. He turned to Sqn Ldr Thomas and said, "Sir, I think that a complete nissen hut is moving up the runway." The squadron leader having previously briefed his colleagues turned around to the young officer and said, "You must be mistaken, we do not see a hut moving on its own up the runway." Immediately the young officer left the mess, no doubt to seek medical advice. This was a huge joke on the station and I was nicknamed Gipsy Lewis. Whilst commuting from Ffestiniog daily to RAF Llanbedr, I would pick up en-route a civilian, I'll call him Big Bill who was employed as a civilian on the station. One morning I stopped to pick him up but his wife said that he was dead. A few days later on passing his house, I saw uniformed police digging up the gardens. I stopped the car further on and enquired from one of the locals. "What gives at Big Bills house?" He replied, "Have you not heard? The police are looking for buried tins of weed killer." The outcome was that his wife was charged with murder after having exhumed her first husband's remains and they found traces of weedkiller. The case made the headlines at the time, but his wife was discharged, due to a legal hitch after her trial.

It was during my stay at my home in Ffestiniog, that I made the acquaintance of a Finnish girl who was the same age as myself and employed on the catering staff of the Finnish Tourist Board and we became engaged. A few weeks later I was called into the squadron leader admin office and was informed that I was to be posted overseas to the Canal Zone in Egypt, to an MT storage unit called RAF EL-FIRDAN, as AIS Inspector (Aeronautical Inspection Services), having previously qualified at RAF Cosford. The tour was to last 2.5 years.

We are now in the year of 1947 and I was to proceed by air passage. It was rumoured that the British Government was withdrawing its troops from Cairo and Alexandria and concentrating its forces on the Suez Canal but to abandon control of this vital waterway to British Commerce was unthinkable. It was also seen as the focus point of our military strength and security in the Middle East and North Africa due to our vast base which had been developed on the West Bank.

One amusing incident that occurred prior to leaving RAF Llanbedr, I must record. Whilst in the squadron leader's office, there was my opposite number present, F.Sgt Lee who was also informed that he too was posted to the Middle East. The poor man turned white and begged to be excused and hurried to his own office.

On arrival at his office, I found Lee, the flight sergeant busy on the phone to command and the conversation was as follows. "Is that you Tosh? This is Phil from Llanbedr. What's all this about my posting to foreign parts? You know that I have a wife and three kids and another on the way.... OK Tosh, I shall leave it to you then." A few days later a signal came through that Lee's posting overseas had been cancelled. When the news came through, he turned to me and smiled, "Wheels within wheels" and tapped his nose and that was that.

The only incident that was unpleasant during my stay at this unit, was the one involving theft. We were paid fortnightly and I always returned to my office immediately after pay parade. I was called out to inspect a tractor which was alongside a Ventura aircraft which was being checked over by a Sgt G. and apart from myself we were the only two personnel in the immediate vincinity. I was called to the phone but I had left my uniform jacket alongside the tractor as it was a very hot day. It contained my wallet and a fortnight's pay.

The aircraft fitter sergeant I noted, on my return, was no longer in the vicinity. I checked my watch and found that it was lunch time. I put on my jacket and discovered that my wallet had gone. I notified the service police and the result was that the sergeant was hauled out of the mess and stripped and searched in the guardroom. The wallet or cash was never recovered but I was firmly convinced that he had taken it. We all knew that he was heavily in debt and if he happens to read this book and has a conscience, then, 'Please donate to charity the amount you stole.'

I left Llanbedr on embarkation leave, together with my posting instructions and a few days later I was on my way to the Middle East by air.

CHAPTER XIII

EGYPT: SUMMARY OF EVENTS

10 Oct 1951	Anti British riots sweep the country following Egypt's decision to rescind its 1936 alliance with Britain.
14 Oct 1951	London: Britain offers Egypt a new defence pact under which Britain would give up its rights to the Suez Canal.
19 Oct 1951	At dawn, British Forces were in control of all the key points on the Suez Canal. No service casualties and only two dead and five wounded Egyptians.
21 Oct 1951	Egypt: Four British warships are now in Port Said and more troops are heading for the Suez Canal Zone. British troops including paratroops landed under the command of General Erskine. The prompt action reflects the rapidly deteriorating situation in the Canal Zone. Britain made a major concession to Egypt, who had been asking for the withdrawal of British Forces, ie a Middle East Pact backed by France, Turkey and the United States of America, which would include a five nation organization. Britain would then hand over her Egyptian base to it. The Egyptian Government rejected the Plan. Rioting broke out in the Zone.
6-28 Nov 1951	Cairo: The Egyptian Government declares a state of emergency. The Egyptians take control of the town of Ismailia. Egypt: British agree to withdraw from three towns if the Egyptians promise to quell terrorism.
4 Dec 1951	British troops of the Royal Sussex Regiment come under Sten and rifle fire from a band of 40 Egyptians near the town of Zuez.

The Egyptian Government give decorations and promotions to the Ismailia policemen who fired on the British Army in the riots there last month.

23 Jul 1952   General Mohammed Neguib of Egypt seizes power in a military coup.

26 Jul 1952   King Farouk of Egypt sails out of Alexandria during the evening in his luxury yacht. He abdicates in favour of his 9 month old son and leaves all power in the hands of General Neguib. There are smiling faces as the playboy King flees amidst cheers.

27 Jul 1952   Egypt and Britian open talks on the future of the Canal Zone.

24 May 1953   Egypt: Britain holds further talks on the future of the Suez Canal.

27 Jul 1954   The 65,000 British troops and airmen, plus 18,000 men of the King's African Rifles are to be pulled out of the Suez Canal Base under an agreement reached today with the successor to be General Neguib, who was ousted from power by Colonel Nasser two years ago in 1952

CHAPTER XIV

EGYPT: RAF EL-FIRDAN CANAL ZONE

The land of Pharoahs and pyramids, dominated by Cairo, a sprawling shambles of a city, perched as it were on the banks of the Nile, with a pencil thin canal, which cuts through the desert, linking Port Said and Suez, the Mediterranean and the Red Sea, the north and the south a channel between the two worlds. King Farouk had become more portly and corrupt and was soon to be overthrown.

On the 23rd July 1952 a group of young officers in Cairo seized power in a bloodless coup, resulting in Farouk sailing away into exile. Amongst the free officers, their leader Colonel Abdel Nasser, waited for an opportune moment to overthrow the ruling 1st President of Egypt from office, General Muhammed Neguib. Abdel Nasser advocated Egypt's future based on socialism and Arab nationalism, whilst the more conservative and religious in temperament, General Neguib, totally opposed Nasser's ideology. In the year 1954, Neguib was accused of having associations with the extremist Sunni Muslim group, known as the Muslim Brotherhood, was arrested and Nasser became President.

Young Egyptians carried out guerrilla attacks against the British bases in the canal zone to force the British army to evacuate, but the British army having lost its base in Palestine, was determined to hang on to the canal zone and it was during these difficult times and extreme violence that Cliff was to witness death and destruction during the height of the power struggle.

The remaining part of the journey into Egypt was by a troop train and here I was to witness the art of bartering. The train was full of service personnel and running alongside the train were several Egyptian hawkers, flogging their wares on a changie for changie basis. There were a few minutes before the train was due out of the station and in my compartment was a corporal by the name of Robinson, an experienced and seasoned veteran of the Middle East.

From my vantage point, one could see the desert, that vast unrelenting, hot, silent golden sand, stretching as far as one can see to the horizon and beyond. The line of vision was disturbed by the odd camel, with its majestic bearing, moving slowly with its rider, dressed in a flowing white galabiya and tilting slightly on the camel's back. Inside the train compartment, there was a thick layer of sand, which one could actually taste, and the fine grains would even get into one's nostrils.

My attention was diverted to Cpl Robinson who was busy at the carriage window flogging duty free tins of woodbines, for watches and lighters. Having completed the transaction, the train was on the move again. As it slowly pulled out of the station I happened to look out through the open window, and running alongside the platform, with howls of anguish, and shaking their fists were half a dozen hawkers, in bare feet, tripping over their dirty galabiyas.

We gathered speed and they disappeared from view and I turned to Robinson and enquired why the hawkers were angry. He smiled and said, "That will teach the bastards a lesson." It transpired that on a previous tour of the Middle East, some of the hawkers had stolen his wallet and during the changie for changie deals, the watches that he received plus a couple of rings, passed off as diamong rings were fakes. The hawkers he explained were masters of the craft and experts at turning out watches, lighters and rings as silver, from worthless metals, which would turn black after a few days and the working parts would fall out after a couple of weeks usage.

Cpl Robinson was an engineer by trade and to pay these characters back in their own coin he had carefully removed all the cigarettes from the tins, by carefully unsoldering the sealed lids, and filling them with paper and a few grains of sand to make up the weight and re-soldering the lids, to their original state.

I was not impressed with El-Firdan, an isolated transport storage unit, the storage compound being run by a British civilian. On the other side of the sandy road, and running parallel to the station was the famous sweet water canal. Lord only knows why this dubious title was allocated to one of the most diseased canals in the world. If one of the British happened to fall in he would be hauled smartly to sick quarters for a series of painful jabs, most unpleasant.

The unit was partly encircled by high barbed wire fence and patrolled by vicious and bad tempered alsatians, under the able control of the service police but more of the incidents involving the dogs, will be retold later.

Opposite the guardroom and situated on the bank of the sweet water canal, was a small brick limed building which housed the miniature power house and would have to be guarded by service personnel in the near future. The senior NCO's living quarters were a row of caravans inside the barbed wire, close to the main road and would be a prime target for the terrorist in the foreseeable future. Those airmen who did not have their families with them, were housed three to a tent, safely situated within the camp boundary. The officers' quarters were in pre-fab wooden huts. The administration block and the various messes were also constructed of wood. The aeronautical inspection staff of which I was soon to become a member, had their office in a caravan and the 'Head of the Department', was a very able warrant officer. For some unknown reason, to the east of the camp, the barbed wire fence was discontinued, leaving the eastern side exposed to the open desert.

Amongst the work force, were several Egyptian engineers, their head was a fellow called Abdul but we were not to know at that point in time that I would later identify him as a leading terrorist and a wily opponent. A few miles from our base was a well organised maintenance unit with solid brick buildings and workshop hangars.

A short distance away was the large army garrison of Moascar, and further afield our nearest town of Ismailiya where the services' club was located under the name of 'The Blue Kettle'. To the west of Ismailiya and on the town's perimeter was the civilian village of Aroshia where large white bricked flats had been recently built, mainly by Greeks, who rented them out at exhorbitant rents, to service families. The rents were subsidised by our government in massive allowances. It was a standard joke amongst the single servicemen that the head of each service family had to collect their pay in wheel barrows, totally untrue of course.

The comradeship here was truly esprit-de-corps and among my friends were F.Sgt Gorman (accounts), F.Sgt B Williams, a master butcher in civvy street and F.Sgt Hewitt, a driver, and a real stirrer who was awarded the wooden spoon. There was one flight sergeant, we shall call him Bates, to whom I had loaned a hundred pounds to bring his wife from England where it was rumoured that she was leading a full sex life at home. It was a callous remark that he made when we were swimming in the Blue Lagoon referring to the hundred pounds he owed me, that so incensed my rescuer that he redoubled his efforts to locate me.
The other friend was a Cpl Washer who was red hot on entertainments and had recently formed a dance band. I was approached to participate as the trumpeter and I gladly accepted. From here, I was invited to join the station military band, where I played the 'E Flat' tenor horn.

My service duties were to inspect and categorise all vehicles. This was a daunting and endless task relieved by the occasional collection or delivery of vehicles and entailing a long journey to and from Port Said to our base. One day I was detailed to deliver a Bedford QL to Port Said, and set off armed with revolver and detailed instructions not to stop under any circumstances until I reached my destination. My journey took me through a small Arab village where the damned truck stalled. A group of Arabs approached the truck and a most agressive character tried to board the cab. It was at this point that I pulled out my revolver and wrapped the knuckles of the nearest Arab. Then sweating cobs as it were, the engine restarted and I quickly pulled away. It was at this point that I had visions of a quick burial in the desert, the truck hidden and vandalised. Delivery of vehicles to Port Said and outlying areas were to be strictly reduced and it was decided that future deliveries would be in convoys.

On Sunday afternoons, transport would be laid on for conveying the dance band to Ismailiya and to the services' club at the 'Blue Kettle'. On the makeshift stage we would assemble to entertain the three services who were off duty. There would be F.Sgt Gorman on the piano, F.Sgt Roberts on the alto sax, Cpl Washer the band leader on the drums, myself on the trumpet and SAC Richards on the string base.

One particular Sunday, whilst entertaining, a fight broke out, involving an unsavoury character, a private in the army by the name of 'S', who jabbed another private in the face with the jagged end of a bottle. As a result the private required several stitches. I remarked to one of the band members that he would come to a sticky end. He was later hung in the hills having been found guilty of the alleged murder of an Egyptian taxi driver in Cairo.

It was the custom of all ranks to visit the Blue Lagoon for swimming and a few of us decided to avail ourselves of this opportunity on the Saturday. We were picked up by service transport and arrived at this highly organised centre, situated a few miles from Moascar Garrison. Positioned a few yards from the shore was a floating pontoon and on it were several SNCO's and airmen, including F.Sgt Bates. I decided to take one of the married familiy's young lads onto the raft, or pontoon and half way across, I realised that I would not make it. I pushed my passenger, young Rodney, onto my shoulders and he was rescued by Sgt Osborne who was sitting on the pontoon. I was not aware that the Blue Lagoon had undercurrents and had claimed many a life. It was a few moments later that I started to swallow water, I panicked and down I went to the murky bed of the Blue Lagoon. The only recollection I have of the incident was what was retold to me later by Sgt Osborne when I awoke in hospital. Apparently, Sgt Osborne was sitting on the pontoon and had dived on two occasions to locate my body but had been incensed by the following conversation on the pontoon. F.Sgt Bates had turned around to Sgt Osborne and said laughingly, "Good effort on your part George, but Cliff has gone so I don't have to pay back the one hundred pounds I owe him." George immediately dived again and in the murky depths saw a white patch being covered over by silt. He had discovered my body and brought me up to the surface. In the next few seconds there was intense activity on the raft/pontoon, with mouth to mouth rescucitation, and somehow I was revived. It is true that in cases of near drowning, one's past is revealed in a panoramic flash and is likened to a fast moving camera film, lasting perhaps a few seconds.

This experience had a traumatic effect on me and thirty years on, I have a deep respect for water and I will never venture out of my depths.

With Christmas looming on the horizon, we decided to relieve the piggery of its remaining occupant, old Joey and we were briefed to assist

F.Sgt B.Williams the civilian master butcher who on demob had decided to carry on with his civilian occupation. There were two pigstys near the sergeants' mess, one containing Joey and the other containing a sow and its piglets. The animals were purchased by the members of the mess and maintained by us. My assistant was Sgt Blower and we entered the sty. Waiting patiently was the flight sergeant with his stunning instrument. My task was to push Joey out and I was on all fours in the confines of his sleeping quarters. I think he knew his number was up and he reluctantly moved to the entrance with a few heart rending squeals.

Unfortunately Williams slipped and in the process only grazed the animal. All hell was then let loose, and Williams cleared the pigsty wall with two feet to spare. Blower was not so fortunate. As he jumped for the wall, the pig grabbed his heel, which was sheared off by the pig's jaws. I was still in the sty and fled for dear life. Later however the pig was despatched in record time and was evenly divided between the three messes.

One incident I must record, occurred in the summer of 1947. The evenings were hot, and it was usual to sleep in our caravans with the doors open, the door aperture being fitted with a light framed mosquito door, which was hinged and independent of the main door. We were warned that if any intruders came to the caravans we were to feign sleeping and let the intruder thieve to his heart's content, and hopefully he would be caught on his way out. The reason for feigning sleep was sound advice as the intruder(s) would not hesitate to slit one throat, especially when one was in the prone position - in bed.

One evening I fell asleep and was awakened by a slight movement and in the moonlight a shadow was observed on the inside of my caravan. I lay perfectly still and squinted at the shadow, as it drew closer. It was a Arab, naked except for a loin cloth. His body was gleaming in the moonlight and there was an overpowering smell of grease which covered him from head to foot. Between his teeth he carried a sharp and evil looking dagger. I could smell his hot breath as he quietly went through my personal belongings, and within seconds he was gone. I quickly put on the lights, jumped out of bed, and raised the alarm. In the powerful searchlight that was suddenly switched on, the intruder was picked up in the beam, the cheeky character was trying to hide on the roof of my caravan. There was a rush to drag him down, but the slippery customer got away, hence the grease and as quick as a flash he was through the point of his entry in the barbed wire, which was found to have been cut. After this episode, security was strengthened and we were again warned to be vigilant and were issued with arms.

One particular guard dog, a vicious looking black alsatian, would grab an intruder if he happened to be in the area on patrol. He would drag them through the wire fence, where the break in occurred and dump them in the sweet water canal.

My prediction regarding private 'S' had at last come true. He was found guilty of the alleged murder of a Cairo taxi driver and was sentenced to hang. The gallows were made at an army garrison and the public hangman had been summoned to carry out the execution. Due to the political situation that existed in the Canal Zone, a request for clemency was refused by King Farouk and 'S' was duly hanged in the hills. Apparently he refused to see his mother during the final moments of his demise and he was asked if he had anything to say to which he replied, "I shall come back and haunt you", to which the executioner replied, "Form a queue son, there are hundreds waiting in the wings."

We are now in the Summer of 1949 and my first tour of duty was coming to an end. We were awaiting repatriation to the UK. I was called into the station commander's office and it was suggested that I stay for a further two years. My first instinct was to decline this so called generous offer as each and every one of us were counting the days to get out of this hell hole. After a few hours of heart searching, I decided to stay.

Terrorism was being stepped up and security was on the increase. All the single SNCO's were detailed to bring in the married families from Ismailiya and Aroshea. We were armed with revolvers and loaded into trucks to carry out the operation. My detail was to evacuate the married families from the town of Ismailiya, and one particular incident, involved the removal of one family from a flat. As we rushed up the stone steps, an Arab terrorist appeared, trying to enter the flat. As there were several cases of rape, and murder, I quickly aimed my revolver and shot the bastard in the leg.

All the married families were safely brought into the military garrison and our mission was accomplished.

We were now in the mid-Summer of 1950 and guard duties had been stepped up to such an extent that guarding became the primary duty. One of the most dangerous duties, was to guard the isolated transport compounds, outside the comparative and collective security of the station proper. I was detailed for such a duty and as guard commander with one corporal and twelve airmen we would position ourselves, within the barbed wire compound. In the early hours the searchlight would be switched on, and the beam would pick out the desert contour. Communications would be made by field telephone direct to the guardroom, by the look out sentry.

This particular barbed wire compound was a favourite with the terrorists and somehow they managed to time the sweep of the searchlight beam and break into the compound unobserved. Armed with tools, they would systematically remove generators, batteries, spare wheels, distributors, ignition coils and other vital components, and having completed their task, would withdraw into the desert and blend naturally with their surroundings. I was determined to be extra vigilant, during my spell of duty and I summoned the guard and impressed upon them to be alert and to deprive these characters of mobility. It was a few hours from dawn that I was summoned by the look out sentry, a very alert young airman, by the name of SAC Jenkins, as he had detected slight movement in the desert. I hurried to the watch tower and in the beam of the searchlight, I detected the outline of at least six Arabs, half submerged in the sand. I took over the searchlight and motioned to Jenkins to call out the full guard, and to be assembled at the base of the tower, under the guard corporal. When Jenkins returned, I ordered him to sweep the area as normal but not to dwell on the outlined figures in the desert.

I detailed the guard to quietly take up strategic positions between the rows of vehicles, and I decided to let the terrorists enter. The one blind spot was the north end of the compound, and it was here that I decided to observe, together with three airmen. One hour later, and in the pale blue light of the moon, there was an audible twang of wire being cut, at the north end and in they came the entire squad, naked, greased up and on all fours.

The three airmen and myself sealed the gap in the barbed wire, and on a predetermined signal, all the compound lights were switched on, including the searchlight beam, with its concentrated light, stabbing the darkness within the compound.

Of the six terrorists, two were caught and taken to the main guardroom and placed in the cells.

Interrogation of the two prisoners failed to produce information, but I hit upon the idea of introducing a live piglet into their cells. One squealing little piglet, borrowed from the sergeants' mess, was placed in one of their cells, after a few minutes, there was a frantic thumping on the cell door, and the outcome was a satisfying question and answer session to the interrogating officer's list of queries.

One day I was summoned to the senior technical officer's office and informed that I was to proceed on a daily detachment to a neighbouring RAF maintenance unit, a distance of approximately five miles from base. My duty there was to manufacture concrete pillars, suitable to form a base for a chassis. The chassis had to be stripped and on to it, a dynamometer was to be installed at one end. It was to be used for the purpose of testing and setting the BHP of engines, which had been overhauled at the unit. Most tests were carried out at 2" fan opening.

It was on one of those days, during testing of a Bedford QL engine, that I had failed to take precautions. I had started the engine, I was dressed in a dust coat, and my RAF tie was flapping about, when suddenly it got caught in the open revolving propshaft. It was only the prompt action of a colleague that prevented a near case of strangulation. My dust coat was in ribbons, my tie had tightened around my neck and my face had turned blue. After this incident, I was ticked off by the technical officer, and henceforth, guards were placed around the open prop shaft. This detachment was interesting, as it involved phase inspections of all aspects of major overhauls etc...

CHAPTER XV

EGYPT: TERRORIST ATTACKS ON BRITISH TROOPS

During 1951 relations between Egypt and Britain were to worsen. Food supplies to the British Canal Base were to be cut off. Egyptian civilian labour was withdrawn, and guerilla attacks were carried out on a more intensive scale by a variety of groups, including the Moslem Brotherhood. In January 1952 we were manoeuvered by terrorists into attacking the police headquarters at Ismailia.

On 23rd July 1952, Nasser seized power with his friend Major General Neguib as his figurehead. A few days later, Egyptian troops surrounded the Ras-El-Din Palace in Alexandria and the same evening the dissolute King Farouk, the last member of the Mohammed Ali dynasty was sent packing and he sailed for the pleasure resorts of Europe with his vast possessions packed in a couple of hundred trunks. Nasser was now Prime Minister and his henchman Neguib was President. One of Nasser's main tasks was to rid the canal bases of British troops and with this in mind he intensified his terrorist attacks against the British installations.

In January 1952, I was detailed to take a Jeep to Ismailia under armed escort to collect two airmen but we never made it. We were approaching the garrison of Moascar when, lined up along the sweet water canal were army tanks with guns trained onto the opposite bank, directly facing the police Headquarters. A young British army officer was standing up in the turret of the leading tank, talking to the police officers through a hand hailer and I distinctly heard an Egyptian voice emanating from the direction of the Chatacol, the main police building, "Go home you English pigs." The army commander replied, "I will give you five minutes to surrender." The five minutes were soon up and the tank guns opened fire, with direct hits on the station, killing forty Egyptian policemen and wounding seventy before the remainder surrendered. This phase heralded the riots in Ismailia where the convent was attacked, the prime target being the wives of servicemen living in flats.

In Cairo it was alleged that British women were attacked and some of them disembowelled and thrown into the streets. British troops were retrieved from the sweet water canal horribly mutilated by the wives of the terrorist mobs. One could only pray 'But for the grace of God go I'.

On return to base I approached my CO and stated that I had overstayed my welcome here and I was three months overdue for repatriation to the UK.

CHAPTER XVI

RETURN TO S OF TT AS MECHANICAL TRANSPORT INSTRUCTOR

At base one of my colleagues, a sergeant Pinder remarked, "If I get out of this alive I shall put in for RAF Weeton and chat up a Blackpool landlady, marry and settle down to running a boarding house." By coincidence he did just that, but more of this later. My posting eventually came through and I was to be posted to RAF Weeton as instructor on mechanical transport. That evening we celebrated in the mess, with a few stellas, the famous onion brewed beer as we nicknamed this portent Cairo brew. Any reference to onions however, is in the imagination only.

My tour of duty now ended in the Canal Zone. I was homeward bound to dear old blighty. Having arrived in the UK, we were to proceed to Weeton, from Euston, via Crewe. After years in the Egyptian desert, surrounded by miles of yellow sand as far as the eye could see, the contrast of the carpeted green of the beautiful English countryside and the gentle slopes of the valleys as viewed from our train compartment, the true meaning of the green grass of home became apparent. We fell silent, each with one's thoughts and the memory of Egypt began to fade.

We eventually arrived at our destination and we wasted no time in settling into the familiar surroundings. This phase of my career was a pleasurable one. My duties were to prepare students for their finals, which embraced all aspects of mechanical transport engineering, prior to their examinations at the 'Trade Standards Centre' at RAF Weeton. Competition between the instructors and the rivalry for the highest number of passes increased the pressure and kept us on our toes so to speak. I had been at RAF Weeton for a period of six months when in the sergeants' mess a new arrival from El-Firdan appeared - no other than Sgt Pinder, who was posted in as a driving instructor.

The social activities embraced a monthly dance at the sergeants' mess of which the main female guests were the Blackpool landladies. In the meanwhile Sgt Pinder had set his sights firmly on one particular pretty blonde, a landlady and a widow. Within a matter of weeks he had obtained a sleeping out pass, became emotionally involved with the landlady and would turn up daily to work in a new car. The net result of his wooing was a marriage and as far as I know he is now a landlord of a prosperous guest house in North Parade Blackpool.

My fiancee meanwhile managed to obtain a transfer as SEN (Senior Enrolled Nurse) nearer to my base at Weeton. On weekends we visited the car mart auctions at Queensferry and would purchase a car, travel up to Ffestiniog to see the old folk, sell the car at a modest profit, come back by train and repeat this lucrative venture on several occasions, with the added advantage of trying out several cars of different makes.

CHAPTER XVII

RAF HENESFORD IN THE MIDLANDS HOLDING UNIT

We are now in the Spring of 1953, and an urgent posting came through to take over the transport section of RAF Hednesford, in the county of Staffordshire, the nearest towns being Cannock and the city of Lichfield.

Cannock was a small mining town on the outskirts of the extensive wooded Cannock Chase, containing deer. Four miles southwest is Hilton Hall, containing the moated home of the Vernons, with a lofty tower in the park commemorating the capture of Portobello in 1739.

Lichfield contains a very fine cathedral of E.E. and Dec. example, and much restored. The three spires form a notable landmark and are known as the 'Ladies of the Vale'. The Lady Chapel contains the 16th century Herkenrode glass. Chantrey's famous 'Sleeping Children' are in the choir aisle. The Close contains some very old houses and also the 17th century Bishop's Palace. Dr Johnson's parents are buried in St. Michael's church with its 15th century tower. St. Chad's church has a very ancient tenor bell.

Royal Air Force station Hednesford was a small unit, with primitive conditions. The sergeants' mess comprised a prefabricated wooden building. The ceremonial square was on a slope with a gravel base. Living quarters were also of the wooden variety. Married airmen were billeted in the surrounding area in the town of Cannock. The station commander, a group captain, was devoid of any sense of humour and a dedicated autocrat, the station warrant officer was of equal temperament.

The CO had the unique ability to dress down SNCO's on parade in front of the airmen, which hardly encouraged morale or discipline.

It was on such an occasion, when on one of his numerous parades, that I was pulled up for the lack of shine of my shoes. I was ordered to report to the S.W.O. in the sergeant's mess the following evening, with the said shoes polished with a mirror shine.

As the shoes were wet, I placed them in the sergeant's mess cook house oven but forgot to remove them. On retrieving the shoes later, I realised that they were totally charred. This meant a quick visit to the clothing stores for a new pair - at my expense.

I duly presented the shoes on a silver platter to the station warrant officer at the mess the following evening and the incident was closed.

It was at this station that I decided to get married to my Finnish fiancee and this duly took place at Lichfield. We managed to obtain accommodation with a very old lady, a widow, and life settled down to domestic bliss as it were.

I received a letter from my parents that they had moved to a town in mid Wales, where Dad had been offered the post of steward of the British Legion Club. We decided to visit them at the earliest opportunity and on one fine Summer weekend we motored down.

Newtown lies on the river Severn and the town itself was noted for its woollen manufacture. The remains of the old church stand near the modern building. Here too, is the 17th century 'Checkers Inn', half timbered and thatched. Newtown also houses the Robert Owen museum, Robert Owen being the founder of the cooperative movement. Here is also the 'Upper Bryn', a fine timbered house dating from 1660.

Newtown was also a close knit community of devout christians and a thriving market town. It boasted a cinema on the banks of the river Severn, ably managed by a colourful character of perfect manners and immaculately dressed with distinguishing features and a bowler hat.

One of the town's main drawbacks was the flooding of the banks of the river Severn when the town would be awash with several inches of water in houses and shops in Broad Street and the surrounding streets. In the future all this was to change with the arrival of the mid Wales development board. Flooding of the town was to be halted by the introduction of a restraining wall. New factories were to be built, the population was to be doubled and trebled.

Near Newtown is the historical village of Montgomery where there are scanty remains of a Norman Castle (AM) from which one can obtain a clear view of the beautiful surrounding countryside. The church is partly E.E. and has a good screen. Seven miles from Montgomery East is the prominent peak of Corndon Hill 1,684ft high, a notable landmark.

CHAPTER XVIII

2ND TAF (TACTICAL AIR FORCE)
RAF OLDENBURG, GERMANY

On my return to RAF Hednesford, I was called into the CO's office and informed that I was to be posted to 2nd TAF (Tactical Air Force), Germany. I was to proceed on my own, pending allocation of married quarters, which was on a points scheme, determined on length of service. As this was my first visit to Germany, I looked forward to the three year posting with anticipation. The station that I had been allocated to was Royal Air Force Oldenburg and my duties were to take over the Mechanical Transport Section.

There was a fine network of autobahns particularly the Bremen roadway which led to the approaches of Oldenburg. The station was laid on a solid foundation of bricks and mortar, ample building provisions had been built into the living and administration blocks to allow for the cold winters, with communal central heating and sealed double glazed windows. There was a practical gap between them and they opened inwards for ease of cleaning. The hinges and securing catches were on a taper to take up any subsequent wear and condensation and heat loss was nil. Double glazing manufactureres in this country, please take note.

The sergeants' mess was of the highest standard and it was alleged that the heavy oak double doors on the entrance, ornately carved with German legends and the swastika had been fitted by Field Marshal Herman Goering. In fact, this was one of his messes and in constant use during World War II.

The next six months proved to be highly rewarding and interesting and after alterations to the existing transport set up, running and servicing schedules were met, by the efforts of a very able and enthusiastic ground staff. It was during this period that I had been allocated a married quarter and I was allowed leave to assist the removal of my personal belongings from our private accommodation in Cannock and to arrange my return with my wife to Oldenburg. Unfortunately the relationships developed with the staff and officers were to come to an abrupt end. I had been at Oldenburg one year, when I was called into the commanding officer's office, a group captain, we shall call him Reeves, a gentleman of the old school an able and just administrator and highly respected by all the station personnel.

CHAPTER XIX

IMMEDIATE POSTING TO A CIVILIAN FIRM
MESSRS A D STRUVERS

"I'm afraid sergeant that we have to lose you, you have been selected by 2nd TAF Headquarters for special duties in Hamburg. The posting is immediate and you are to proceed to a civilian firm, called Messrs A D Struvers, of Gros-Borstella-Strasse on Aeronautical Inspection duties." I was to be the sole inspector there to carry out stage and phase inspections on what was then a revolutionary aircraft refueller, called the Buckeburg which had incorporated in the design a special coupling now known as the Avro Hardol coupling, an ingenious device which, when coupled to the aircraft fuel tanks, would gradually close down as the back pressure from the fuel tanks increased on filling, thereby eliminating spillage and risk of fire.

When I informed my wife that we were to move to Hamburg the next morning, she was not too keen at that time, as my eldest son John the first in the family was only three months old. He had been recently born in Germany at RAF Rostrup hospital.

We were allocated a beatle back Volkswagen of the service variety in drab green with the RAF roundel insignia and having handed over our married quarter we loaded my son in his carry cot onto the back shelf on the Volkswagen. It just fitted. Having said our numerous farewells we left this happy unit for the unknown as it were and motored onto the Bremen autobahn for the long journey to Hamburg.

Our accommodation had previously been organised from Oldenburg in a block of civilian and British service flats at Listrasse, in view of the beautiful red church with its distinctive tower and only a few minutes walk to the shopping centre of Hamburg. Our flat was a large one on the second floor, with three bedrooms, large lounge, bathroom, and kitchen.

It was a strange feeling taking up abode amongst German civilians who for all we knew were former and dedicated Nazis. However time proved me wrong. They were perhaps subdued and distant, but later they revealed themselves as ordinary citizens, correct in manner, friendly and amiable. Much later one of the families invited us in for coffee and in broken English, showed photographs of their two young sons in military uniform who had been killed and their parents who had perished in the allied bombing of Hamburg. Such is the horrors of war and the useless loss of human life, where humanity was just another statistic filed in the archives of the Nations.

Having settled in I reported to the Director of the German Firm of Messrs A D Struvers armed with service schedules and official return certificates for the attention of the technical officer at 2nd TAF on completion of the monthly quota of refuellers for the services usage within the command.

I had been allocated an office on the higheset point of the administration building, with a commanding view of my empire as I called it. I had been at Struvers for approximately six months, when I had my first visit by a squadron leader from Headquarters. He arrived one morning and he looked vaguely familiar and without further preamble, wasted no time in introducing himself. He was no other than the ex-warrant officer from East Anglia and the nasty incident on my promotion to sergeant in preference to his own selection sprung immediately to mind. His opening gambit was as follows.

"You have done alright for yourself, with a cushy posting to a civilian firm," and I immediately replied, "With due respect, Sir, you have done better." From then on he was a constant visitor to the firm, perhaps he enjoyed my company, or more likely, the excellent dinners laid on by the firm and the vintage wines.

One amusing incident involved a test run on one of the refuellers, prior to issuing as fit for service use. During the slow run through Hamburg, I noticed that some of the German pedestrians were staring at my vehicle, smiling and waving as I passed. It was only when I glanced through the rear mirror, that their laughter was justified. Unfortunately I had steered my vehicle onto the sacrosanct tram lines and behind me were two trams following at a respectful distance. Red faced and acutely embarrassed, I quickly accelerated off the rail track.

Hamburg is a beautiful and bustling city. The ravages of war had left deep scars but bombed sites were rapidly being cleared and high rise buildings could be seen in various stages of erection. There was the Rhine with its broad expanse of water with various ships going about their business and sailing amidst the ships were various pleasure boats. In Hamburg itself was the famous Reepabahn with various clubs, packed with local residents and tourists enjoying the various live shows, and perhaps some of the seedy ones. One of the clubs worthy of a visit is the Moulin Rouge, which caters for all tastes. One day in the Autumn I received notification that my seconded civilian posting was coming to an end, as the contracts for the refuellers were dwindling to zero. The following week the post came to an abrupt end and I was informed that I was to complete my tour with a posting as AIS (Aeronautical Inspection Services) to an RAF station under the name of Royal Air Force Bruggen, to the maintenance transport servicing unit. Married quarters had been organised so that was one headache disposed of.

RAF Bruggen is situated on the Dutch border between Roemond and the small village of Elmpt. Within a few kilometres was 2nd TAF

Headquarters, based at Rheindalen and nearby was the town of Munchen Gladbach.

Royal Air Force Bruggen was a vast and busy complex. All the buildings were ultra modern and constructed of bricks and mortar. Service personnel had been trained to carry out their duties to the highest standards. They were capable of turning out immediately in the event of a red alert.

This too was in the main a happy station and the morale was high. Married quarters were a neat row of large terraced houses and each individual quarter had its own central heating, fired by coke boilers, located in neat white washed cellars under each building. In emergency such cellars could be used to accommodate the odd bed or two.

My next door neighbour was a Sergeant Thompson who I discovered later was to be one of my colleagues at the MTSU.

I reported in to my officer commanding that unit, a squadron leader who we shall call Baker. He ruled the unit with a rod of iron and his direction leaned towards the 'Autocratic' type of leadership.

I was one of the few SNCO's who managed to weigh him up and he was particularly benevolent towards me.

As a senior inspector in charge of inspecting vehicles and stamping the authorisation of vehicles fit for service use for distribution, there had to be a mutual respect and a deep understanding of the smooth running of the unit. It was essential not to rock the boat too hard.

The only biggest drawback of this posting, was the repetitive Red Alerts. Our contribution was to organise the several hundred vehicles into convoys and drive them on pre-determined routes through Germany, followed by spells under canvas.

I decided to join the station band. This was to prove a shrewd move on my part as one of the perks was to be excused station duties such as orderly sergeant and living under canvas during alerts.

My next door neighbour and colleague, Sergeant Thompson related how his father, a close friend of a gentleman by the name of Spencer, was given the opportunity in a joint venture, for the sum of one hundred pounds each, to open the first store, which later was to prove to be a highly organised, chain of stores throughout the country - now known as Marks & Spencer. My colleague did not mention why his father declined the offer and remarked that it could have been Thomson & Spencer.

One day I was called into my commanding officer's office and he informed me that I was to take a serviceable radio vehicle to Ulm, a distance of a few hundred kilometres from our base. The journey there was uneventful but it was on the return journey that the trouble started. I was to return with an SAC driver in an RVT vehicle which was due for overhaul and in conversation on our return journey it transpired that he had very limited experience in driving that kind of vehicle and as this tour was his first abroad, he was slightly nervous. As many a seasoned traveller knows, in that part of the world, the journey from Ulm back to base can be a nerve wracking experience. The road was devoid of crash barriers, with a drop of several hundred feet to the valleys below and whilst negotiating the various bends, the driver began to sweat cobs, to use an RAF expression and I decided to take over the helm as it were. I ordered him to pull over and I took control. We travelled through the night and at dawn we were nearing the village of Elmpt, a few miles from base. By this time I was bleary eyed with fatigue when suddenly the vehicle veered off the road and carreered into the back yard of a farm.

The washing line was full of the weekly clothes, which we found draped around the cab. The vehicle's front end was embedded in a haystack and the cab was full of chickens. We were unhurt, but it was only then that it dawned on me that I had broken a few rules. Firstly I had taken over the vehicle without authorisation, in as much that the sacred F295, the official driver's document, did not include my name as second driver and was not certified by the transport officer.

The other important factor was that the damage to the vehicle, although of a minor nature, would warrant in any event, a FMT3, which was the official form for reporting traffic accidents within the service. Also there was a slight case of compensation to the farmer, if he decided to claim. Later at base I was hauled up to the OC of the unit and was formally charged and during the hearing, I was asked if I would accept the CO's punishment, or elect a Court Martial. I opted for the CO's ruling, and was fined £25 and an entry in an otherwise clean service record.

We were now celebrating the pre Christmas celebrations at the unit and the squadron leader, our CO, requested that I report back to his office after the remainder of the section had been dismissed. "Take a seat, Sgt Lewis, and have a drink. I think I overreacted to that incident of yours, and I have only recently been told by the official driver of the vehicle, that he could not carry on driving the vehicle as he was extremely nervous of heights. There is nothing I can do to remedy the situation, but you were guilty of infringing the regulations. However you

are due for repatriation to the UK and I shall ensure that you have a special recommendation from me on the amount of work that you have done here and it will be to your immediate advantage with your promotion."

CHAPTER XX

RAF BLETCHLEY AND RAF STANBRIDGE
BUCKINGHAMSHIRE

It was in January of 1957 that my posting came through to a small unit at RAF Bletchley in Buckinghamshire. I was to take charge of the servicing side of the transport section where my opposite number, a W.O. Scott, was in charge of the driving side a gentleman of the old school, humorous, but slightly devious in a friendly sort of way.

I had been at the unit for a period of a few months, when we were informed that the unit was closing down and that we were to be transferred to a larger unit under the name of Royal Air Force Stanbridge, only a few miles away from Leighton Buzzard, a town that lay on the river Ouzel and which boasts of several old inns and a restored 15th century market cross.

I was allocated married quarters at RAF Stanbridge which were extremely comfortable and modern. I had been at this station only a matter of weeks when I was called into the station commander's office. His first words were, "Sgt Lewis, you are improperly dressed." I squinted at my No.1 uniform. The crease in my trousers was there, buttons were polished, my head gear was at the correct angle and my shoes were highly polished. He repeated the statement once more, but with a difference. This time he mentioned Flight Sergeant Lewis, with a smile, and the penny dropped. I had been promoted and after the usual congratulations, I wasted no time in obtaining my crowns from the clothing stores. A few weeks later I was posted to RAF Digby in Lincolnshire, a thriving signals unit.

CHAPTER XXI

RAF DIGBY, A SIGNALS UNIT IN LINCOLNSHIRE

I was to take over the whole of the transport section, the driving side and the maintenance side. Under my command would be twelve civilian drivers, service drivers and the maintenance staff. Royal Air Force Digby was yet another happy unit. The station commander, a wing commander, by the name of Seymour, proved to be an officer and a gentleman of the old school, strict but fair, and he earned the respect and trust of all who served under him. My immediate superior to whom I was responsible was the CTO (Chief Technical Officer) by the name of Wing Commander Hancock, another gentleman of the old school who proved to be a good friend when things became tough.

Married quarters were a row of very old terraced houses, but comfortable and were located outside the station. Ours was in Cuckoo Lane. Perhaps some of the old veterans who were stationed there, will remember the road. Today the quarters stand empty and a recent nostalgic visit brought back many happy memories of the station as it used to be in the fifties.

Royal Air Force Digby is strategically positioned for socialising. The city of Lincoln is approximately 17 miles to the north and the town of Sleaford a mere seven miles to the south.

Lincoln lies on the river Witham with the old town rising from the north bank, with the cathedral at the summit. The Newport Arch is a relic of the walled Roman city, the former Lindum Colonia.

The cathedral, 11th to 15th century has a fine west front with stately triple towers of which the central tower is a grand example of 14th century architecture. At the east end is the famous Lincoln Imp. One of the cathedral's greatest treasures, is the best of the four existing copies of Magna Carta.

The town of Sleaford boasts a church, 12th - 15th century with a tower and spire rising to 144ft. Amongst the old buildings is the vicarage dating back to 1568. The 'Black Bull Inn' preserves a carved stone dated 1689 and depicts bull baiting.

As Royal Air Force Digby was in an isolated spot, I formed a committee for the purpose of exploring the possibility of a motor club on the station, to cater for the servicing and maintenance of members' private cars, during off duty periods. A disused building was set aside for the project and a grant was obtained from the Lord Nuffield trust fund for the purchase of garage workshop equipment. This project escalated to embrace cycle training for the children of the married families, which eventually led to proficiency certificates issued by

69

'RoSPA' and from here and in close co-operation with the constabulary of Sleaford, road safety was introduced. I wish to thank the chief constable of Sleaford for the ample supply of material and films which I used on the many lectures I gave both to the civilians and service staff at the station.

I had been approximately eighteen months at Digby when the tranquility of my section received a jolt, in the form of a young pilot officer, who we shall call Plt Off Prune. Apparently he was fresh from the officers' training college and his secondary duty was to take over the MT section as officer in charge. I remember vividly the day he introduced himself and by natural instinct I came to the attention, saluted, and from that moment, I realised here was an officer, egoistical and full of his own self importance.

During conversation he emphasised that he knew nothing of mechanical transport but was there to pick my brain so to speak. I saw very little wrong with this approach. At least it was an honest admission and I decided to cooperate fully with him, but things began to go drastically wrong within a few days.

We were expecting the AOC that is the Air Officer Commanding the Group on the general annual inspection of the station and this gave us the opportunity to 'Bull Up' the sections, dispose of the accummulation of rubbish, steam jenny the hangar floors, and to paint everything that did not move in brilliant white paint. We were busy on these tasks, when Plt Off Prune rushed into the section in a panic and entered my office. "F.Sgt Lewis, I want you to go through all the service manuals relating to the MT," (of which there were many). "I found a comma missing. I want you to insert any commas that are missing, and enter it as an amendment and sign as having done so." "With due repect, Sir, should this not wait until after the AOC's visit as we are up to our necks in it?" "F.Sgt, this is an order and I want to see all the volumes tomorrow." This was at 5pm, knocking off time. "Very well," I said, "if you insist." His parting shot was, "Do not forget the Sir when you address an officer of the Realm."

The great day arrived and we were standing in readiness for the cavalcade that would eventually arrive at my section.

All the vehicles not in use were in review order in the hangar, the airmen were in clean overalls, NCOs and civilian staff were in dust coats and the coaches were spruced up outside in immediate readiness for the transportation of personnel to and from the station. Plt Off Prune arrived in his No.1 uniform and he called me to one side and said, "F.Sgt I shall walk immediately behind the AOC during the inspection and I will answer all the technical questions." I said to myself, "We shall have some fun here before the day is out." "Very well Sir," with emphasis on the Sir. This did not go unnoticed by the little upstart.

The great moment came and the cavalcade arrived preceded by the station commander and followed by our CTO, the chief technical officer.

The AOC began inspecting the vehicles in the hangar, where all the vehicles had their engine bonnets up, in order that the he could check for engine cleanliness. One of the vehicles to be inspected was a new addition to the station, a Volkswagen, and in this instance, only the boot was open which acted as a luggage compartment and was situated at the front.

The AOC turned to Plt Off Prune and asked, "What is this vehicle on, Mr Prune?" He took a quick look and said, "Engine change, Sir." The AOC went to the rear of the vehicle and said, "What is this engine for." The reply was, "That is the replacement engine Sir." The AOC was not amused and a much chastened Plt Off, realising his error, tried to flannel his way out of that one, which made matters worse.

Apart from this incident all went well and we had an excellent report from the AOC. Matters between the Plt Off and myself however, came to a head and I requested a move. A few days later the Plt Off was posted but I carried on, and the section was back to normal once again.

CHAPTER XXII

RETURN TO RAF BRUGGEN 1962. VISIT BY HRH PRINCESS MARGARET, VISCOUNTESS OF SNOWDEN, 1964

In the summer of 1962 I was called into the central registry and informed that I was to be posted abroad. To my delight it was back to Royal Air Force Bruggen in Germany, to fill a warrant officer's post as MT Controller. My family in the meantime would remain at Digby until married quarters were allocated at Bruggen, which normally would be within a period of three months.

On my arrival at Bruggen, I found that there had been several major changes particularly in my previous section. I duly reported to the MT officer who we shall call Flt Lt Bloggs. The impression I received of this balding gentleman was of a man slightly around the bend, which became more apparent as time went by. My office was next to his and both our offices were bogged down with piles of bumph, to use an RAF term. The amount of paper work emanating from his office would give credit to the civil servant establishments throughout the UK. Official directives would be interspersed with his own amendments and annotated in pencil. Morale was low and charge sheets were the highest within the station. Also jankers using RAF slang for withdrawal of individual privileges where airmen have to carry out menial fatigues as directed by the service police were frequently dished out.

One day I was called into the MTO's office and sitting at his office desk was a very happy officer with his new toy which was in the form of a control panel, hastily installed over the weekend and fitted with a series of buttons which interconnected with the various senior non-commissioned officers' offices within the administrative building.

The object of this infernal machine, became apparent almost immediately. Whenever he wished, he would press some buttons which would result in a buzzer sounding in the respective offices which meant a general rush in the direction of the 'Augustus presence' namely to the MTO's office. Unfortunately the buzzers sounded simultaneously in each office and having mustered at the main office, the MTO would point at the SNCO who he would wish to consult and the remainder would disperse. The buzzer would sound several times throughout the day.

One regular event which was embarrassing to the senior staff was the odd behaviour of the MTO who would remove his head gear and throw it out through the open window and then select a SNCO to retrieve it at the double.

On the lighter side, the domestic scene and the social life on the station were excellent. During a dance at the sergeants' mess one

Saturday evening, we were honoured by the presence of selected members of the 'Chelsea Pensioners' that fine body of men, resplendent in their uniforms.

My family had recently joined me and the married quarters were better than the previous one.

I made up my mind that if I was to survive this tour under an MT officer whose embarrassing loss of control was becoming more and more evident as time went by, I had to humour him. He had the ability and flair of delegating practically all the workload, which in my view was a good thing and a challenge. As time went by I became more or less his personal aid, but there was an element of friction and a clash of personalities in our relationship.

One amusing incident occurred during a spot of leave. We as a family decided to go camping and we selected the Hook of Holland as our destination. We left RAF Bruggen on a brilliant summer's day and having arrived at our camping site, we pitched our tent on a slope of the sandy ground. Next to our tent was a smaller tent, occuped by a German and I think, his Frau.

The evening passed quietly with a visit to the camp club. We then settled down to what we thought would be a peaceful night. There was an ominous quiet, and suddenly around 3am there was the howling of the wind followed by a heavy downpour of rain. We were in the middle of a hurricane and in the light of my torch, I saw my neighbour's small tent disappear with a frightened couple in their birthday suits, huddled together. The male was shouting 'Godfordoma.' That morning we hurriedly made for the car and shelter and we left almost immediately. That was the end of my first camping experience.

The remainder of the holiday was uneventful and we arrived back at base to discover that the weather had been exceptional with continuous sunshine.

Back at the section I discovered that the MTO was becoming difficult to handle and his behaviour was becoming more and more erratic and unpredicatable.

We were preparing for the visit of 'Her Royal Highness', the Princess Margaret, Countess of Snowdon, who had graciously consented to visit Royal Air Force Bruggen on the 15th July 1964 to present the standards to Nos 80 and 213 squadrons. This was to be Her Royal Highness's second visit to Bruggen the last occasion being when returning by air from Germany to England exactly ten years previously on 15th July 1954.

A squadron qualifies for the award of a standard after 25 years of service. Such a presentation is therefore a rare honour and a highlight in the lifetime of most service personnel. We were most fortunate on

73

this occasion to be able to witness a dual squadron standard presentation.

Perhaps at this stage it would be appropriate to mention the history of Royal Air Force Bruggen which is one of a clutch of four RAF airfields, situated between the Rhine and the Maas. These airfields were all built during the expansion of Nato Forces in the early fifties. Bruggen was completed in July 1953 only twelve months after the first tree was cut down.

The history of RAF Bruggen can be roughly divided into two periods, 1953-57 when it operated as a fighter station and 1957 to the present day during which time it has been basically a Canberra station.

During the fighter phase of Bruggen's existence, No 23 squadron, the Belgian Air Force and Nos 67, 71, 112 and 130 squadrons, operated for varying periods from RAF Bruggen. No 55 RAF Regiment Wing and No 5004 Airfield Construction Wing also served at the station during this period, while the General Equipment Park or No 431 Maintenance Unit as it has been known since 1960, is the only unit to have served continuously at Bruggen since the station opened and where I had the honour to serve for two overseas tours. During its comparatively short existence, RAF Bruggen has been honoured by three Royal visits, with His Royal Highness, The Prince Philip in 1958 and His Royal Highness The Duke of Gloucester in 1960.

It was with a sense of relief that we heard over the grapevine that our MTO had been posted and was due to leave in the next few days. His replacement proved to be yet another gentleman with vast experience in handling men, and was to prove to be a very able and respected officer. It was in March 1965 that my tour of duty came to an end and reluctantly I made plans to return home.

I had purchased a 17M Taunus Ford vehicle and a bluebird caravan from new and I was fortunate to have had the vehicles for the requisite time in Germany to avoid any UK duties that would have been otherwise imposed by the 'Customs & Excise'.

CHAPTER XXIII

RAF LYNEHAM, WILTSHIRE

My posting was to a major flying station in Wiltshire, namely Royal Air Force station Lyneham and having arrived with my family, where married quarters were at a premium, I obtained permission to park my caravan on the outside perimeter of the airfield, on farmer's land, overlooking the local cemetry and station. As we had arrived late, there was no point in booking into the new station until the following morning.

The next day I was up early to book in, and report to my section and the MTO. It was here that I nearly suffered a heart attack. My MTO was no other than Flt Lt Bloggs of my former unit at Bruggen. "I was expecting you F.Sgt Lewis, what took you so long?" I was speechless and it took a few minutes to regain my composure. I listened to his rambling on about workload, running a large section with no warrant officer, (which meant that all the responsibility would be mine), and about the efficiency of the smooth running of the station. The sergeants wasted no time in making their views of our mutual friend known. It was at this station that I decided to quit the service on premature discharge. One of the deciding factors was as follows. The MTO would be away most of the days and would instruct me to return, after working hours at the section, to brief him on the day's events and to go through a stack of files, requiring his signature. I could not return to my quarters until the late hours. One day he decided to go on yet another of his frequent leaves with a repetition of his after duty visits in the evenings.

It was during this period, having applied for discharge, that I contacted the Regent Oil Company of London, now known as Texaco and was interviewed by a Mr Chambers. I was successful in obtaining the tenancy of a new but untried filling station and garage a few miles from Lyneham in the ancient town of Devizes. We had already purchased a house at Devizes so my civilian future seemed rosy.

Looking back at 30 years in the Royal Air Force which now seems only a fleeting moment in time, and a highly rewarding career, and now at the age of 65, and retired, one cannot help but dwell upon the memories of a bygone era. Today with the sophisticated, complex computerised weaponry and technology within the Royal Air Force, surely this is a challenge to younger generations, and worthy of a career to maintain peace and render us safe in this blessed land called 'Britain'.

To the Royal Air Force, the caring and elite Force, to my former colleagues, officers and friends, I salute you.

The appendices relate to a few true anecdotes submitted by former colleagues and are of general service interest.

APPENDIX A

Len Bridge
Author

Newtown-Powys-Mid-Wales, May 1982

During 1943 my squadron, No.200, were stationed inland of Bathurst in the Gambia, at RAF Yum Dum, equipped with Liberators MK IV, and engaged on anti-submarine, 'Search & Strike'.

One morning our CO received a signal from Command to move the squadron to St. Thomas Mount, Madras in India. Within two days the entire squadron were on their way with the exception of my own crew and skipper, who being a flight commander, had been given the task of handing over the airstrip to an oncoming company of Royal Engineers.

This procedure took some two weeks, after which we followed the squadron to India, via Tarkodi, Lake Chad and across central Africa to Wadi Seidna near to Khartoum and then on to Wadi Halfa for a night stop and further refuelling. Several hours in the air took us over the great Aswan Dam and then over the valley of the Kings at Luxor and whilst flying low to see the valley of the Nile, we flew into a cloud of locusts, which forced us down at El-Fasher, a medium sized airstrip. We were held up for two days to clean out the air intakes and oil coolers before proceeding to Cairo west.

We stayed at this resort for four days, during which time we took a tram trip out to Giza to see the great Pyramids and the Sphinx.

Whilst in Cairo we were given yellow fever injections, and dust screens fitted to the air intakes of the aircraft.

We left Cairo west for Bahrain in the Persian Gulf and after a brief stay, we had the long haul to Karachi. On arrival we were informed that the Liberators were being impounded and that we would have to avail ourselves of whatever transport was available to get across to Madras in Southern India, a distance of 1,250 miles as the crow flies. Our first lift was to Delhi and the whole crew loaded into a Hudson aircraft. On arrival we slept at a disused army camp with the dubious title of Delhi Lines. Not being provided with mosquito nets, we were badly stung. The infernal mosquitoes were well educated and would hover, switch off engines, and dive on the appropriate target.

Our squadron leader, by the name of Cliff Wescombe, by arrangements with an army unit, obtained transport which took us to a very large island with a lake covering several hundered acres. On its bank, was a magnificent Hindu Temple, now derelict and had been taken over by the Royal Air Force as a Sunderland flying boat base, with a couple of Sunderlands beeing moored out on the lake, with motor boats being used to get out to them.

The skipper of the Sunderland informed us that they were awaiting the arrival of a very distinguished VIP who we had to ferry to another inland lake on an island near to Hyderabad. It was suggested that we join the flight as it would knock several hundred miles off our original journey to Madras. Unfortunately he was unable to convey how long we would have to await the arrival of the VIP, who was travelling by road. We had very little food and had to exist on stale biscuits and lime juice. To kill time we managed to obtain a football, which we kicked around for five hours. Sitting on the temple steps and completely exhausted was a certain WOP/AFs Johnny Johnson, a typical cockney, who had dropped off to sleep. At this stage the skipper revealed the identity of the VIP, no other than Marshal Chiang-Kai-Czek.

Suddenly there was a cloud of dust and three cars drew up, carrying high ranking Chinese officers and their entourage. We were called to attention, with a guard of honour, consisting of four erks, with three rifles and one pick handle. As the Marshal drew level with us, whilst inspecting the impromptu guard of honour, Johnny Johnson audibly exclaimed: "To think that we have been starving all day, and kicking a bloody ball around for nearly five hours, waiting for a slant eyed git!"

Early in 1942, my unit, 264 Squadron were moved to RAF Colerne on the outskirts of Bath and were re-equipped with Mosquito aircraft for night fighter duties. As a result of this, any free time forthcoming had to be taken during daylight, with an early return for the night flying stint for which it was possible to avail ourselves of station transport that may be running.

One morning my oppo. Bill Bailey suggested that instead of going into Bath, we should essay the walk into the town of Chippenham, a few miles away. It was now early Summer and a sweltering hot day of tropical temperature and dressed in RAF blue, and perforced to carry our respirators and tin hats we set off. We trudged along in the sweltering heat of the hot summer's day, with the hope that something or other would come along and give us a much desired lift. This was not to be however, and perspiring, we at last dragged our weary limbs into Chippenham. Our first thought was for something to eat and drink so calling into the nearest pub we settled down to bread, cheese and the inevitable pickles and a couple of pints. We had a couple of hours left and the time came to trudge back to Colerne.

We were two miles from Chippenham, when we caught up with another erk and were carrying on to our base, when our newly formed companion remarked, "Eh chaps, there is a car coming." With this, we started thumb swinging, in the hope of a lift, but to our dismay the car, a magnificent black Daimler, chauffeur driven with his companion, also in uniform, disappeared around the immediate bend. As we approached the bend, we observed that the Daimler had parked at the edge of the road and the chauffeur was making his way towards us. He said that although he was not going into Colerne he had been directed to give us a lift. As we approached the car, we were told that we would be sitting in the tonneau at the rear, with no other than HRH Mary, the Queen Mother. We were also told that whoever spoke first was to address her initially as 'Your Royal Highness' and subsequently, to call her 'Ma'am'.

She was very charming and graceful making us feel very much at ease as she engaged us in easy conversation.

We had travelled thus for little more than a mile when she called her driver through the car's communicating tube. The car was brought to a halt and I heard HRH say, "It is about half a mile back on the left hand side of the road."

The car was immediately turned around and after travelling a short distance, HRH instructed the driver to stop. "It is somewhere about here in the hedgerow." The second chauffeur left his seat and instructed us to join him. We were walking through the long grass and weeds when the second chauffeur said, "HRH has seen some scrap metal in the hedgerow, which she requires us to collect." We were now knee deep in thistles, nettles, and dock leaves searching for what we discovered were two very old and rusty barrel hoops. It took all four of us a good fifteen minutes to disentangle them from the very thick undergrowth during which we all suffered nettle stings and at the same time got ourselves and our uniforms covered in red rust. Our prize was then stowed away in the luggage boot of the Daimler and the chauffeur explained that the Queen Mother collected scrap metal as part of her war effort. We remained in the car for another couple of miles when the car came to a halt, at the entrance to a drive, leading to a large country house, where we learned that the Queen Mother had been evacuated to from London.

On our return to base we reported to our sergeant, as we were a bit late for flight duties and we tried to explain the condition of our uniforms etc, that we had been riding in the country with the Queen Mother. There was a slight pause and the sergeant bellowed, "You shower of bloody liars, you had better think up another one."

APPENDIX B

Submitted by: Ex Warrant Officer R.S.Angell, No.968942, Flight Engineer, Coastal Command, Royal Air Force, and now retired and living in Newtown Powys Mid Wales.

At times Ack Ack guns were sited in coordination with the Royal Air Force during the war years. A gunner had recently been posted to us from the south coast and during conversation, stated that his previous detachment had been well respected by all and sundry until the day of misadventure dawned. They fired and hit one of our own aircraft, the famous Wimpey, or Wellington bomber. From then on, the local school children having heard of the incident decided to re-route their homeward path, which passed near to the offending gun pit on the airfield perimeter. They had loaded their school bags with stones and numerous rocks. Taking careful aim, they would direct their missiles with deadly accuracy at the unfortunate gunners. This form of retaliation was more effective, than any field punishment which may have occurred.

One day I was posted to a regiment and later was informed in general conversation with a gunner of an incident which occurred at a gun pit.

A lone hostile aircraft, a Dornier, had appeared over one of the gun pits, and at that time, a minimum crew was manning the guns.

The sergeant in charge was drinking tea with the remainder of the detachment about four hundred yards away, in one of the billets.

Hearing the sound of gunfire, the sergeant dropped his mug of tea and ran towards the gunpit, thinking that the gun crew had weakened the fighting strength of the RAF Fighter Command. He stumbled across the path of the troop captain who had rushed from T.H.Q. With the enemy out of sight the sergeant said, "Please say it was a Dornier Sir, and not one of ours that has been hit," and the captain replied, "It was a Dornier, Sgt Wiliams." Much relieved , Sgt Williams obtained a full report from the gunners at the pit. The gunner remarked that the bloody gun had jammed and managed to fire the one and only shot that hit the Dornier.

At a later date, there came to the now famous gun site, a visiting 'General', where the gun crew, headed by Sgt Williams, stood to attention on parade, with the sergeant beaming with joy and pride. The General said, 'Congratulations men', and turning to Sgt Williams, asked, "Why only one shot sergeant?", and quick as a flash the sergeant replied, "There was only one Dornier, Sir." This remark was duly noted and was published in the 'Brigadier Magazine' under the heading of ONE SHOT WILLIE. The gun pit referred to was located at Bognor Regis.

I was fortunate to witness the following incident. Enemy fighters had appeared overhead and two lone Spitfires appeared from nowhere. On seeing the Spitfires, the enemy fled. The Spitfires were out of ammunition and were on their flight path back home. Such was the bravery of the few and I dedicate the following poem, to those gallant pilots.

THE FEW

They were the young
They were the brave
They fought just for us
Their country they saved

To this day I look up
To the clouds and the sky
To think of the young ones
The brave ones that died

The battles they fought
No cost did they count
Duty to do was their only thought
For their King and Country
So bravely they fought

Their loved ones they suffered
They suffered such pain
They stood there in silence
They stood there and prayed

Just to see once again
The loved ones they knew
They were the ones we call the few

The Battle of Britain
That Battle of fame
They were the young ones
They were the Brave

Composed by Alwyn R Scammells, Ex Royal Regt of Artillery

JUNO BEACH

The dawn had not long broken
On this a beach of sand
Juno they did call it
The place where we did land

Men had gone before us
And bravely they did stand
They held their lines unbroken
For us to safely land

Friend and foe, fought bravely
Fighting hand to hand
This was just their token
For their beloved land

We who still remember
Will always understand
Why we do remember
Our comrades in the sand

Our silent thoughts unbroken
In silent prayer we stand
They gave their lives so freely
For this, their loving land

Juno Beach they called it
The place where we did land
Juno Beach they called it
The beach of crimson sand

Composed by Alwyn R Scammells, Ex Royal Regt of Artillery

APPENDIX C

Note from Cpl Robinson : Engine fitter, East Wretham

I was regarded as a casanovah and with this distinguishing trade mark, three of my comrades and myself decided to visit the town of Bury St Edmunds. We arrived and visited the 'Sally Ann', that famous voluntary organisation, which catered for the well being of servicemen. For the sum of nine pence, we sat down to a meal of fried bread, egg, bacon, and beans and a mug of tea followed by afters, namely dundee cake. I, in the meantime was carefully eyeing the local talent and one beautiful blonde serving behind the counter of the canteen, caught my eye. I excused myself from my companions and quickly made for the counter with the pretext of purchasing fags. My three colleagues remarked, "Robbie is at it again."

I approached the counter and after a few exchanges made a date to meet this vivacious girl the following evening. At the appointed hour I was outside the Sally Ann waiting patiently for my dream girl. She eventually turned up but I was not amused. Complete in Salvation Army uniform, bonnet and book, she smiled brightly and said, "Take my arm. We have another convert I see, and we are just in time for an outdoor meeting. You can participate." Needless to say this was the last time I saw the young lady. I went back to camp very early, a much chastened young man.

APPENDIX D

My turn to join the ranks came in 1946 just after the war. After leaving school at the age of 14, I worked underground in the slate mines of Blaenau Ffestiniog, with a sound knowledge of service life, picked up from my father, who joined in 1939 in the voluntary Royal Welsh Fusiliers, at Newtown. My eldest brother Cliff had been in the RAF a few years and my other brother Jack a few years later and also in the RAF. I decided to enlist in the RAF at Padgate then down to Yatesbury in Wiltshire, 'Square Bashing' as we termed it. I enlisted as armourer's assistant, which allowed plenty of time to follow my favourite sports of boxing and running. From Yatesbury, it was Thorney Island in Hants, with visits to Portsmouth, Emsworth etc. I was extremely keen to go on an overseas tour and prior to this I met up with Cliff my eldest brother in Newtown. He used to buy old bangers and would bring them home to Newtown to flog. I purchased from him such a banger, namely an old square bodied Rover for £38, a princely sum in those days. One day we went fishing and my partners were Jim Purnell, Frank Roberts and a foreigner by the name of Ches. On taking a left hand bend outside Carno, I looked in the mirror, and saw a wheel following us down the road and realised that one of our back wheels had come off. We came out of it without injury and had a bit of a laugh, when we pulled up. The car fell on its hub with all the fishermen in the back falling on top of each other. When told to Cliff, he replied, 'A case of overloading, brother'.

My overseas posting came through at last, to Japan, with the occupation forces. I had the usual embarkation leave then joined the troopship Dunera, at Southampton. We travelled through the Bay of Biscay, the Mediterranean, Suez and stopped at all the ports for fuel and water. After six weeks we docked at Kuve harbour in Japan, then we travelled by train to Iwakuni, not far from Hiroshima where we joined Forces with the Kiwis and Australian Air Forces. The posting proved a pleasant and rewarding one and it was time to go back to the UK after a three year tour. We sailed back on the sister ship of the Dunera, namely the Dilwara. The only incident that occurred was as follows:

A person had fallen overboard. No one knew at the time until a passenger saw a body floating in the water. The ship circled and a boat was lowered. Then there was yet another of those inexplicable miracles. The body was that of a small girl and although she was unconcious she was alive. Moments later the weather deteriorated with a heavy swell. The captain remarked that if she had been found later she would have drowned.

Today, I wonder what has happened to her.

Submitted by: Les Bridge of Newtown, Powys, Mid Wales.

It was in 1937 that I arrived at RAF Driffield on my first posting to a unit, 51 (B) Squadron. I had completed my aircraft apprenticeship training at RAF Halton in December but had been detailed to return to Halton after Christmas leave to join a team to supervise the new recruits - the 35th entry. I had discarded my green cap band for the black band of an airman and so started my twelve years man service. The new recruits reminded me of myself, being put on the London train at Newcastle by anxious parents and actually meeting a fellow recruit there and setting off at least with someone for company. He was obviously a musician - carrying a large guitar. When the train stopped at Durham station, a gentleman walked into our compartment, followed by a boy who he introduced as his son 'Fred'. "Are you going to RAF Halton?", he enquired, and on replying in the affirmative we were asked to keep an eye on Fred.

It turned out that Fred and I became firm friends and it transpired that he already had older friends at RAF Halton. It also transpired that he was always slightly ahead of me in most of our tasks and never required any supervision.

My first posting was to RAF Driffield - Unit 51 (B) Squadron was equipped with 'Virginia Bombers' - twin engine bi-planes. These aircraft seemed massive to me but there was ample room in the newly built hangars specially designed to accommodate such aircraft. I was allocated to 'B' Flight under a Flight Sergeant known as 'Jeffrey' who was short in stature.

Many of my fellow fitters and riggers were long service airmen adorned with three good conduct stripes similar to to-days technicians, the only difference being that the long serving airmen had their stripes reversed on the bottom part of their sleeves. I am sure that these old timers would have a lot of tales to tell about their long service careers both at home and abroad.

During this period and as an incentive, promotion to corporal on the NCO's ladder would eventually lead to a further 12 years service. My first test was to be taken onto the starboard wing of one of these monsters and I was instructed to turn the engine. It was a sort of proficiency test. Having ascertained that the switches were in the 'Off' position, I engaged the starter dog with the button on the cowling and having inserted the starting handle, I turned the engine over. I had won my 'Spurs' as it were and knew the procedure! When the aircraft were in the hangars and the birds were roosting, this necessitated the cleaning of these large wings so high up. Keeping to the footmarks along the spars was a precarious task. One of the 3 G.C. badge fitters, we shall call him Spike was a carefree character. With his aircraft outside 'Chiefy's' office door, he called out, "Yoo Hoo Jeffrey!" The indignant Flt Sgt came to the door of his office shaking his fist at the miscreant and said, "If I come up there I'll......" (unrepeatable). That airman whose name alludes me attained his ambition to become an Observer and was posthumously awarded the VC when he and his pilot flew their aircraft into a bridge held by the enemy, where previous air strikes had failed to destroy it. Although there were large hangars at Driffield in 1937 the new barracks were still under construction so we were billeted in those long huts heated by two round cast iron stoves, with their metallic pipes sticking through the roof of the huts to remove the smoke from the stove. In the winter we were glad to secure all the blankets we could scrounge and had a very cold walk to the outdoor ablutions, it was mostly cold water.

The station W.O. (Warrant Officer) was a stickler for ceremony and the square must have been laid out at an earlier date. Each morning we lined up in working blue for colour hoisting under the command of very junior officers. The tirade from the S.W.O. is unprintable and made the junior officers in command 'Blush'.

By Easter 1937 we began to convert to Avro-Ansons and 'B' flight took over the Ansons, while 'A' flight kept the 'Jinnies', the nickname given to the Virginia Bombers, 51 Squadron. 51 Squadron then moved to Boscombe Down, a well established RAF Station, the only drawback was that the hangars were small compared to those at RAF Driffield, so the housing of the 'Jinnies' became a careful manoeuvre because of the wing tips and unfortunately Fred's Jinnie suffered damage.

Our problem in 'B' flight was solo pilots doing circuits and bumps, forgetting to lower the undercarriage although it took 250 turns of a handle alongside the pilot's seat to raise it. Such a landing entailed lifting onto trestles, lowering the undercarriage and then towing to the hangar for repair, plus changing two airscrews which were well and truely bent, after checking the propellor shaft and changing the pitot head. It was at this stage that I undertook training as an Air Gunner and was unpaid until qualified. This I hoped would be my first step up the ladder to Sgt Pilot - the ambition of most apprentices who failed to obtain a cadetship to RAF Cranwell.

The first entry in my log book reads and I quote:

> 6.9.37 1030hrs Anson T.K6277
> Pilot Sgt Bickenson and Plt Off Holloway
> Cross country and photography.
> Base Portland Bill Newtown Abbey.
> Filton Base 1400hrs.

I had on occasions flights in the Virginias doing camera gun air to ground attacks from the rear turret. In February 1938 51 Squadron took delivery of the first Whitley and I had the honour to be fitter in charge.

I well recall proudly surveing this aircraft 'U' for uncle K7226 one Saturday morning. It was parked on the tarmac and I had done the daily inspection when along came Plt Off Gilchrist in civvies, in the company of the CO, Wg Cdr Riversdale Elliot, who had spent the previous week on a navigation course in London. The Plt Off enquired if the Whitley was ready for flight. I quickly got the F700 signed and replied, "Ready for flight, sir", and he said that the CO also wished to fly and asked me if I would like to accompany them. I agreed and ran for my parachute and harness.

The flight was over Portland Bill and Hartland Point, with me sitting in the wireless operator's seat in overalls. The aircraft was a front line bomber prior to the outbreak of War, with one free gun in the rear turret. Very quickly they were modified, with however a Vicker's 'K' gun in the front turret, a retractable turret in the centre fuselage and a 4 gun hydraulic turret in the tail.

Submitted by: 566844 ACI A V Thomas 1937-1939, later Flt Lt, Engineering Officer of Bomber Command.

AT NEWTON WE PUBLISH New Author's books and also SELL THEM... Recent releases:

"A WALK WITH GIANTS". Bill McEwan has an unusual story to tell from his time with the Army in France, the evacuation from Dunkirk, remustering to the RAF, shot down in the Channel and captured by the Wehrmacht. His three years experiences in POW Camps. Return to UK, difficult times, hard work and move to Africa. The problems of involvent in the countries with their change to Independance. It is highly informative and enjoyable narrative. The Foreword is by **Bill Reid VC, BSc.** ISBN 1 872308 18 X, SB. Price £15.95

"ASPECT OF ANXIETY" by Dr T V A Harry MB, Ch.B (Manc), DPM., This is an eminently readable book covering anxiety, a normal response to stress a psychiatric and physical illness. The book encompasses an enormous breadth of material including manifestations and treatment, giving a well balanced view of the dependency problem. There are also useful chapters on self-help and the techniques of relaxation. The literary style is delightful and scholarly. A work well worthy of a small space on the bookshelves of most doctors and anyone with an interest in problems associated with anxiety. ISBN 1 872308 27 9. SB. Price £6.95.

"BLACK SWAN" by Sid Finn A history of 103 Squadron. From formation prior to WW1, peacetime, WW2, operations in the Far East to the final disbandment, a worthy record. Foreword by Air Chief Marshal Sir Hugh Constantine, KBE,CB,DSO,LL.D. ISBN 1 872308 00 7. HB. Price £14.95

"BOMBERS MOON" Victor Minot the author, an ex Bomber Command air gunner on Wellingtons and later a pilot writes from a position of strength. The tale is based on actual experiences of the author, and by fictionalising a romantic element which becomes part of the story, illustrating the considerable effect on morale of the women they left behind. "Bombers Moon" reflects the fact that more than two out of every three aircrew lives in Bomber Command ended in death in action. Foreward by Air Vice Marshal F C Hurrell CB,OBE,FRAeS. ISBN 1 872308 67 8. SB. Price £14.95

"BY THE SEAT OF YOUR PANTS!" Hugh Morgan's diligently researched investigation into the training of WWII pilots under the Empire Training Scheme, BFTS, Arnold and Towers Schemes, in South Africa, Rhodesia, Canada, and USA. Foreword by Air Marshal Sir John Curtis, KCB,KBE,FRAeS. ISBN 1 872308 03 1, HB. Price £14.95.

"COMBAT AND COMPETITION" by David Ince, DFC,Bsc. A fascinating story of a gunnery officer turned Typhoon pilot. Operating with 193 and 257 Squadrons through the summer of 1944 to the bitter end of Hitler's dying Reich. As a trained test pilot, the author marketed advanced flight control systems. He is a dedicated glider pilot, chief instructor, active in sailplane development testing and a past member of the British team squad. Foreword is by Air Chief Marshal Sir Christopher Foxley-Norris, GCB,DSO,OBE,MA,CBIM,FRSA. ISBN 1 872308 23 6. HB price £15.95, SB £14.95.

"ESCAPE FROM ASCOLI" by Ken de Souza of 148 Squadron. His vivid and fascinating tale of survival in the desert, against the odds. His escape from PG70 Italian POW camp, operating with the SAS and final get-away from Occupied Italy. Foreword by Air Chief Marshal Sir Lewis Hodges, KCB,CBE,DSO,DFC. President of the RAF Escaping Society. ISBN 1 872308 02 3. HB. Price £12.95

Con..2 over..

"DEATH OR DECORATION" Ron Waite's fascinating story of a pilot from from day one of his training, through to operational missions and beyond. His six years of war with No. 76 Squadron, 1658 and 1663 HCUs makes enthralling reading. Foreword by Wg Cdr P. Dobson, DSO,DFC,AFC, (CO No 158 Squadron). A jolt to the memory for those who were there...A seat in the cockpit for those who were not! ISBN 1 872308 08 2. Price HB £14.95, SB £13.95.

"FAITH, HOPE AND MALTA GC" The author is Tony Spooner, DSO, DFC. The foreword by Air Marshal Sir Ivor Broom, KCB,CBE,DFC**,AFC, himself an ace Malta pilot. It is the gripping story of the Ground and Air Heroes of Army, Air Force and Navy defenders of the George Cross Island. ISBN 1 872308 50 3. Price £16.95.

"FEAR NOTHING" David Watkins accurate history of 501 (F) County of Gloucester Squadron, Auxiliary Air Force. The 'part-timers' were in action from May 1940 over France followed by the Battle of Britain. Later re-equipped with Spitfires, Tempests and the Vampires. Foreword by Wg Cdr K.MacKenzie, DFC,AFC,AE. ISBN 1 872308 07 4. HB. Price £14.95

"FOLLOWING THE RED ARROWS ON A WING AND A PRAYER" The author, Carol Turner has been an enthusiastic supporter and has worked alongside the team in its charity caravan at appearances from Dorset to Scotland at the various Air Shows. If you are interested in what the aces are like on the ground, if you want to know what it is like to be part of the RAF's greatest team of Ambassadores. This is the book for you. Illustrated with black and white and full colour photographs and drawings by the author. A beautifully produced hard back, excellent value and a must for the Fans. ISBN 1872308 HB, Price £11.95.

"GREEN MARKERS AHEAD SKIPPER" by Gilbert Grey. Aged 15 at the outbreak of WWII the author had completed a tour of 34 operations serving as a Flight Engineer with 106 Squadron before his 20th birthday. Foreword by Wg Cdr MMJ Stevens, DFC,RAF(Ret'd) who comments: "What a wonderful book for passing on to posterity because it describes what it was really like being a member of the aircrew in a Lancaster bomber in 1944." ISBN 1 872308 11 2, SB. Price £15.95.

"IN FULL FLIGHT" by Tony Spooner DSO,DFC. The author takes the reader from those pioneering days of the famous flying club at Brooklands with its colourful galaxy of brilliant unpredictable youth, to the grim unrelenting mixture of horror and heroism of the Malta blitz. Excellently told, a narrative made additionally attractive by memories of the comaraderie that existed in the RAF Volunteer Reserve. This simple but absorbing tale will prove a tonic in terms of both achievement in the past and hope for the future. Foreward by Air Chief Marshal Sir Hugh Pughe Lloyd. ISBN 1 873454 05 8, HB. Price £14.95

"NO FUTURE" by Des Hawkins DFC. A fictional tale based on the author's real experience as a crew member, one of Sir Arthur Harris' 'Old Lags' flying with Lancaster heavy bomber squadrons 44 (Rhodesian), 630 and 625. It is the fascinating story of a particular crew, their operations over enemy territory, their restricted social life together with the romantic element and a total unexpected final tragedy. Exceptionally perspicacious foreward by Sqn Ldr R C B Ashworth RAF(Ret'd). ISBN 1 872308 10 4, HB. Price £15.95

Available ex-stock, cash with order, post free UK, add £1.90 for overseas;
NEWTON BOOKS P O Box 9, BARRY, S. Glamorgan CF62 6YD.
Tel & Fax 01793-641796